International High School OSSD Teaching Series

国际高中
教学丛书

总主编 赵军武
主　编 桑　妮
副主编 李恩蓓
编　者 付伊宁

12年级数据管理
MDM4U

北京语言大学出版社
BEIJING LANGUAGE AND CULTURE
UNIVERSITY PRESS

图书在版编目（CIP）数据

12年级数据管理 / 桑妮主编；李恩蓓副主编；付伊宁编. -- 北京：北京语言大学出版社，2024. 12.（国际高中OSSD教学丛书 / 赵军武总主编）. -- ISBN 978-7-5619-6676-1

Ⅰ. G634.413

中国国家版本馆CIP数据核字第20244YZ229号

国际高中OSSD教学丛书·12 年级数据管理

GUOJI GAOZHONG OSSD JIAOXUE CONGSHU · 12 NIANJI SHUJU GUANLI

责任编辑：胡学卉
责任印制：周 焱
排版制作：北京创艺涵文化发展有限公司

出版发行：北京语言大学出版社
社　　址：北京市海淀区学院路15号，100083
网　　址：www.blcup.com
电子信箱：service@blcup.com
电　　话：编辑部　010-8230 0358
　　　　　发行部　010-8230 3650/3591/3648
　　　　　北语书店　010-8230 3653
　　　　　网购咨询　010-8230 3908
印　　刷：北京市金木堂数码科技有限公司

版　　次：2024年12月第1版　　印　　次：2024年12月第1次印刷
开　　本：787毫米×1092毫米 1/16　　印　　张：9
字　　数：149千字
定　　价：128.00元

PRINTED IN CHINA
凡有印装质量问题，本社负责调换。售后 QQ 号 1367565611，电话 010-82303590

International High School

OSSD Teaching Series

国际高中

教学丛书

12年级数据管理

MDM4U

序

　　党的二十届三中全会指出，教育、科技、人才是中国式现代化的基础性、战略性支撑；要推进高水平教育开放，加快建设高质量教育体系，统筹推进育人方式、办学模式、管理体制、保障机制改革，办人民满意的教育。习近平总书记也指出，要全面贯彻党的教育方针，完善教育对外开放战略策略，统筹做好"引进来"和"走出去"两篇大文章，有效利用世界一流教育资源和创新要素，使我国成为具有强大影响力的世界重要教育中心。

　　在中国式教育现代化过程中，国际高中已经成为我国高中教育体系的重要组成部分，为推动中国式现代化发展和科技进步，提供了系统性的国际化人才培养渠道，培养了一大批具有国际视野和德才兼备的国际化人才。然而，目前中国境内的国际高中在扎根中国大地办教育，既保证国际化又保证本土化方面，特别是在具体办学和教育教学全过程中，仍缺乏一系列既符合中国国情、能够发挥中国高中学段的教学特色和优势，又能帮助高中生在国外主要教育体系中获得所需学分的本土化教学用书。

　　为了满足我国国际高中的本土化教学需求，我们邀请多名国内优秀的国际学校教师编写了这套"国际高中 OSSD 教学丛书"。他们熟悉国际高中教育体系，教学经验丰富，培养了上千名升入世界著名大学的学生。另外，我们按照学科类别，邀请加拿大著名高中的持牌教师对每本教学用书进行了审读，确保教学用书能覆盖国际高中针对各科学分设计的每个知识点，这对学生学业能力的提升具有很强的辅助性和指导性。

这套丛书首期共出版十册，分别为：

1.《11 年级英语》(ENG3U)

2.《12 年级英语》(ENG4U)

3.《12 年级国际商务基础》(BBB4M)

4.《12 年级数据管理》(MDM4U)

5.《12 年级高等函数》(MHF4U)

6.《12 年级微积分》(MCV4U)

7.《ESL 英语 C 级》(ESLCO)

8.《ESL 英语 D 级》(ESLDO)

9.《ESL 英语 E 级》(ESLEO)

10.《12 年级读写技能课》(OLC4O)

北语留学服务中心在筹划编写本套丛书的过程中得到了众多业内专家学者的支持、鼓励和建议，丛书的出版也得到了北京语言大学出版社的大力支持。在此，谨对参与丛书策划、主编、编写、编辑等工作的同志们付出的辛勤劳动表示诚挚的谢意！同时，北语留学服务中心作为北京语言大学的全资直属机构，在丛书的编写过程中也得到了学校相关学科专家的鼎力支持，在此一并表示感谢！我们也期待丛书的出版对国内国际高中的高质量发展能起到积极促进作用。

赵军武

2024 年 8 月于北京

前 言

　　MDM4U（12 年级数据管理）是大学高级统计课程的基础课程。本课程与数据管理相关，能够增强学生对数学的理解。学生将运用组织和分析大量信息的方法，解决概率和统计的问题，并结合统计概念和技能进行最终的调查。学生还将完善在高级数学中取得成功所需的数学方法的使用。计划进入大学学习商科、社会科学和人文学科课程的学生会对这门课程特别感兴趣。[①]

　　本书旨在帮助学生完成 MDM4U 的学习，将从事需要统计学基础知识的职业的学生可以使用本书作为辅助工具来帮助他们学习。本书内容包括术语的定义、重要概念、示例、公式、图表，以及值得注意的细节。

　　使用本书，学生应该能够对数据管理有一个整体的理解，并掌握解决相关问题所需的技能和技巧。

---

① Ministry of Education of Ontario. *The Ontario Curriculum, Grades 11 and 12: Mathematics* [M/OL]. Toronto: Queen's Printer for Ontario, 2007: 111-122 [2024-04-29]. https://www.edu.gov.on.ca/eng/curriculum/secondary/math1112currb.pdf

Preface

MDM4U (Mathematics of Data Management, Grade 12) is a fundamental course for advanced statistic classes in university. This course broadens students' understanding of mathematics as it relates to managing data. Students will apply methods for organizing and analyzing large amounts of information; solve problems involving probability and statistics; and carry out a culminating investigation that integrates statistical concepts and skills. Students will also refine their use of the mathematical processes necessary for success in senior mathematics. Students planning to enter university programs in business, the social sciences, and the humanities will find this course of particular interest.[1]

This book is aimed at helping students with the learning process of MDM4U. Therefore students who would like to pursue a career which requires the basic knowledge of statistics could use this book as a supplementary tool to assist them. This book includes definition of terms, important concepts, examples, formulas, graphs and charts, and details worth paying attention to.

Using this book, students should be able to demonstrate a general understanding of data management, and are expected to master skills and techniques necessary to solve related problems.

---

[1] Ministry of Education of Ontario. *The Ontario Curriculum, Grades 11 and 12: Mathematics* [M/OL]. Toronto: Queen's Printer for Ontario, 2007: 111-122 [2024-04-29]. https://www.edu.gov.on.ca/eng/curriculum/secondary/math1112currb.pdf

目　录

Table of Contents

OSSD

MDM4U

第 1 单元

必备知识复习

Unit 1

Review of Prerequisite Knowledge

必备知识

在进入本课程之前，学生需要掌握一些数学知识才能取得成功。这些知识包括：

- **运算顺序**：BEDMAS（括号、指数、除法 / 乘法、加法 / 减法）。

- **指数运算法则**：$x^a \cdot x^b = x^{a+b}$，$\dfrac{x^a}{x^b} = x^{a-b}$，$\left(x^a\right)^b = x^{ab}$。

- **解方程**：使用不同的方法求出 x 的值。如果有两个方程，求出 x 和 y 的值。方法包括图像法、代入法和消元法。

- **线性方程图**
  - 线性方程的三种不同形式：标准式、点斜式、斜截式。
  - 线的斜率：$\text{斜率} = \dfrac{\text{上升高度}}{\text{水平距离}} = \dfrac{y_2 - y_1}{x_2 - x_1}$。
  - 如果两条直线平行，则其斜率相同。如果两条线垂直，则其斜率互为负倒数。
  - 学生应能根据图形上的已知点找到直线的方程。

Prerequisite Knowledge

Before the students step into this course, there is some mathematical knowledge that students need to master in order to be successful. The prerequisite knowledge includes:

- Order of Operations: BEDMAS (Brackets, Exponents, Division/Multiplication, Addition/Subtraction).

- Exponent Laws: $x^a \cdot x^b = x^{a+b}$, $\dfrac{x^a}{x^b} = x^{a-b}$, $\left(x^a\right)^b = x^{ab}$.

- Solving Equations: Find the value of x using different ways. If there are two equations, find the values of x and y. The methods include graphing, substitution and elimination.

- Linear Equation Graphs
  - Three different forms of linear equations: standard form, point-slope form, slope-intercept form.
  - The slope of the line: $\text{slope} = \dfrac{\text{rise}}{\text{run}} = \dfrac{y_2 - y_1}{x_2 - x_1}$.
  - If two lines are parallel, their slopes are the same. If the two lines are perpendicular, their slopes are negative reciprocals.
  - Students should be able to find the equation of a line with known points on the graph.

OSSD

MDM4U

第2单元

计数与概率

Unit 2

Counting and Probability

对学生的期望

学生应该能够算出离散样本空间中的事件或事件组合的概率。学生还应该能够运用排列和组合以确定一个事件的概率。[1]

Expectations for Students

Students are expected to solve problems involving the probability of an event or a combination of events for discrete sample spaces. Students should also be able to solve problems involving the application of permutations and combinations to determine the probability of an event.[2]

---

[1][2] Ministry of Education of Ontario. *The Ontario Curriculum, Grades 11 and 12: Mathematics* [M/OL]. Toronto: Queen's Printer for Ontario, 2007: 111-122 [2024-04-29]. https://www.edu.gov.on.ca/eng/curriculum/secondary/math1112currb.pdf

— 第 1 课 —

概率概论

🍁 2.11　什么是概率?

概率是对事件发生的可能性的度量。它衡量的是事件的确定性,可以用分数或百分比来描述。在统计学中,概率代表一个随机事件的结果的可能性。学生可以通过实验的方式理解概率,例如从袋子里抽彩球、旋转转盘、掷骰子等。

🍁 2.12　统计学中的"事件"是什么?

在概率论中,事件是随机实验的结果或定义的结果集合。随机实验所有可能结果的集合称为样本空间,因此事件的另一个定义是样本空间的任何子集。例如,当我们掷骰子时,事件是数字 1 到 6。

🍁 2.13　实验概率和理论概率

实验概率的定义是事件实际发生的概率。事件 A 的实验概率的计算公式可以用分数表示:

$$P(A) = \frac{事件A发生的次数}{试验的总次数}。$$

如果一个公平的骰子滚动了 10 次,而数字 6 出现了 2 次,那么骰子滚动后出现 6 的实验概率计算方式为:

$$P(数字6) = \frac{2}{10} = \frac{1}{5}。$$

理论概率与实验概率不同。理论概率可以定义为有利结果的数量除以可能结果的总数。事件 A 的理论概率计算公式可以用分数表示，即

$$P(A) = \frac{n(A)}{n(S)},$$

其中 $n(A)$ 表示事件空间中的元素数量，$n(S)$ 表示样本空间中的元素数量。例如，我们抛一枚硬币时得到正面的理论概率计算方式为：

$$P(正面) = \frac{1}{2}。$$

离散样本空间的每个结果的理论概率加起来为 1。学生应该记住概率之和为 1。

🍁 2.14　模拟

我们可以使用基于技术的模拟模型来增加试验次数以接近理论概率。课堂活动包括从袋子里取弹珠及旋转带有不同标签的转盘。

🍁 2.15　补集

学生应该确定一个事件的补集，以及两个或多个事件是互斥的还是非互斥的。集合 S 的补集（写作 S'）由样本空间中不属于集合 S 的所有结果组成。

$$P(S') = 1 - P(S)$$

我们可以通过公式确定两个事件是独立的还是不独立的。若满足下列条件，则事件 A 和 B 是独立的：

$$P(A \cap B) = P(A)P(B)。$$

— Lesson 1 —
Introduction to Probability

🍁 2.11　What Is Probability?

The probability is the measure of the likelihood of an event to happen. It measures the certainty of the event. It can be described as a fraction or a percentage. In statistics, probability stands for the possibility of the outcome of any random event. Students can understand probability through experiment, for example, drawing colored balls from a bag, spinning a spinner, tossing a dice, etc.

🍁 2.12　What Is an "Event" in Statistics?

In probability theory, an event is an outcome or defined collection of outcomes of a random experiment. Since the collection of all possible outcomes to a random experiment is called the sample space, another definition of event is any subset of a sample space. For example, when we toss a dice, the events are numbers 1 to 6.

🍁 2.13　Experimental Probability and Theoretical Probability

The definition of experimental probability is the probability of an event actually happening. The formula for calculating the experimental probability of event A can be expressed as a fraction, which is

$$P(A) = \frac{\text{the number of times } A \text{ occurs}}{\text{the total number of trials}}.$$

If a fair dice is rolled 10 times and the number 6 occurs 2 times, then the experimental probability of a 6 on a given roll of the dice would be calculated as:

$$P(\text{number } 6) = \frac{2}{10} = \frac{1}{5}.$$

Theoretical probability is different from experimental probability. Theoretical probability can be defined as the number of favorable outcomes divided by the total number of possible outcomes. The formula for calculating the theoretical probability of event A can be expressed as a fraction, which is

$$P(A) = \frac{n(A)}{n(S)},$$

where $n(A)$ represents the number of elements in the event space, $n(S)$ represents the number of elements in the sample space. For example, the theoretical probability of getting a head when we toss a coin can be calculated as:

$$P(\text{head}) = \frac{1}{2}.$$

The theoretical probability of each outcome of a discrete sample space adds up to 1. Students should remember that the sum of the probabilities is 1.

🍁 2.14　Simulations

We can use technology-based simulation models to increase the number of trials to approach the theoretical probability. Activities in class can include drawing marbles from a bag and spinning a spinner with different tags.

🍁 2.15　Complement

Students should determine the complement of an event, and whether two or more events are mutually exclusive or non-mutually exclusive. The complement of a set S, written as S', consists of all outcomes in the sample space that are not in set S.

$$P(S')=1-P(S)$$

We can determine whether two events are independent or dependent by formula. Events A and B are independent if:

$$P(A\cap B)=P(A)P(B).$$

—— 第 2 课 ——
概率表示法

🍁 2.21 集合表示法

在数据管理中，我们需要使用集合表示法来表达事件空间或样本空间。例如，我们可以将抛硬币的样本空间表示为

$$S = \{正面, 反面\} 。$$

$n(S)$ 表示集合内元素的数量。集合内的每一项称为一个元素。

🍁 2.22 交集和并集

集合 A 与集合 B 的交集是集合 A 和集合 B 中共有的元素的集合。交集表示为 $A \cap B$。

集合 A 和集合 B 的并集是属于集合 A 或属于集合 B 的元素所组成的集合。并集表示为 $A \cup B$。

🍁 2.23 维恩图

维恩图是一种图形表示形式，用于表示不同集合之间的关系。

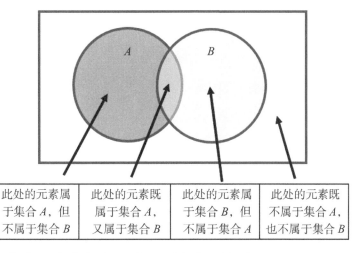

此处的元素属于集合 A，但不属于集合 B	此处的元素既属于集合 A，又属于集合 B	此处的元素属于集合 B，但不属于集合 A	此处的元素既不属于集合 A，也不属于集合 B

如果两个集合不共享任何元素，则它们不相交。

$$A \cap B = \varnothing$$

🍁 2.24 容斥原理

容斥原理的公式：

$$n(A \cup B) = n(A) + n(B) - n(A \cap B) 。$$

例子：

如果 $A = \{3, 4, 5, 6, 7, 8\}$，$B = \{6, 7, 8, 9\}$，

那么 $A \cap B = \{6, 7, 8\}$，

所以 $n(A \cup B) = n(A) + n(B) - n(A \cap B) = 6 + 4 - 3 = 7$。

可以计算两个数据集合的并集的概率：

$$P(A \cup B) = \frac{n(A \cup B)}{n(S)} 。$$

🍁 2.25 互斥事件

如果事件 A 和事件 B 不相交，则它们被视为互斥。

$$n(A \cup B) = n(A) + n(B)$$

— Lesson 2 —
Probability Notation

🍁 2.21   Set Notation

In data management, we need to use set notation to express an event space or a sample space. For example, we can express the sample space for tossing a coin as

$$S = \{\text{head}, \text{tail}\}.$$

The value of $n(S)$ is the quantity of elements within a set. Each item within a set is called an element.

🍁 2.22   Intersection and Union

The intersection of set A with set B is the set of elements that are in both set A and set B. The intersection is denoted as $A \cap B$.

The union of set A and set B is the set of all elements that are in either set A or set B or both. The union is denoted as $A \cup B$.

🍁 2.23   Venn Diagrams

Venn diagrams are graphical representations that are used to show the relationships between different sets.

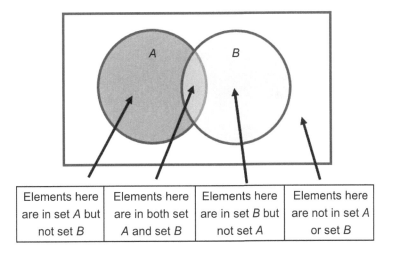

Elements here are in set *A* but not set *B*	Elements here are in both set *A* and set *B*	Elements here are in set *B* but not set *A*	Elements here are not in set *A* or set *B*

If two sets do not share any elements, they are disjoint.

$$A \cap B = \varnothing$$

🍁 2.24　Principle of Inclusion-Exclusion

The formula of inclusion-exclusion principle:

$$n(A \cup B) = n(A) + n(B) - n(A \cap B).$$

Example:

$$\text{If } A = \{3, 4, 5, 6, 7, 8\}, \ B = \{6, 7, 8, 9\},$$

$$\text{then } A \cap B = \{6, 7, 8\},$$

$$\text{and thus } n(A \cup B) = n(A) + n(B) - n(A \cap B) = 6 + 4 - 3 = 7.$$

The probability of the union of two data sets can be calculated:

$$P(A \cup B) = \frac{n(A \cup B)}{n(S)}.$$

🍁 2.25　Mutually Exclusive Events

If event *A* and event *B* are disjoint, they are considered mutually exclusive.

$$n(A \cup B) = n(A) + n(B)$$

— 第 3 课 —
条件概率

🍁 2.31 什么是条件概率？

条件概率是指某个事件或结果在另一个事件或结果已发生的情况下发生的可能性。它一般被表述为 A 已发生的条件下 B 发生的概率，写作 $P(B|A)$，其中 B 的概率取决于 A 发生的概率。条件概率的公式为：

$$P(B|A) = \frac{P(A \cap B)}{P(A)} \text{。}$$

例子：

一个袋子里有 2 个蓝色的弹珠、3 个黄色的弹珠和 5 个红色的弹珠。假设一个人取出一个不是红色的弹珠，那么这个弹珠是蓝色的条件概率是多少？

$$P(蓝色|不是红色) = \frac{P(不是红色 \cap 蓝色)}{P(不是红色)}$$

$$= \frac{2/10}{(2+3)/10} = 0.4 = 40\%$$

🍁 2.32 条件概率的乘法定律

利用条件概率的公式，我们可以重新整理方程来求解交集概率问题。

$$P(A \cap B) = P(B|A)P(A)$$

例子：

计算从一副标准牌中抽出一个国王，接着又从剩下的牌中抽出另一个国王的概率时，实际上是在计算两个事件的交集的概率：(A) 从有 4 个国王的52 张牌中抽到一个国王；(B) 从剩下的有 3 个国王的 51 张牌中抽到另一个国王。

$$P(A \cap B) = P(B|A)P(A)$$
$$= \frac{3}{51} \times \frac{4}{52} \approx 0.0045 = 0.45\%$$

— Lesson 3 —
Conditional Probability

✤ 2.31 What Is Conditional Probability?

Conditional probability is the possibility that an event or outcome occurs given that another event or outcome has also occurred. It is often stated as the probability of B given A and is written as $P(B|A)$, where the probability of B depends on that of A happening. The conditional probability formula is

$$P(B|A) = \frac{P(A \cap B)}{P(A)}.$$

Example:

There are 2 blue, 3 yellow and 5 red marbles in a bag. Given that one draws a marble that is not red out of the bag, then what is the conditional probability that the marble is blue?

$$P(\text{Blue}|\text{Not Red}) = \frac{P(\text{Not Red} \cap \text{Blue})}{P(\text{Not Red})}$$

$$= \frac{2/10}{(2+3)/10} = 0.4 = 40\%$$

✤ 2.32 Multiplication Law for Conditional Probability

With the conditional probability formula, we can rearrange the equation to solve the problem of the probability of an intersection.

$$P(A \cap B) = P(B|A)P(A)$$

Example:

When we calculate the probability of drawing two kings in a row from a standard deck of cards if the first is not replaced once drawn, we are actually working out the probability of the intersection of two events: (A) drawing a king from 52 cards with 4 kings, and (B) drawing another king from the left 51 cards with 3 kings.

$$P(A \cap B) = P(B|A)P(A)$$
$$= \frac{3}{51} \times \frac{4}{52} \approx 0.0045 = 0.45\%$$

— 第 4 课 —
树形图和结果表

🍁 2.41 什么是树形图？

树形图是一种将给定情况下所有可能的结果和概率可视化的方法。树形图也称为决策树，它们可用于绘制相关事件的可能结果。在树形图中，树的每根"树枝"将流程中的一个想法或步骤与可能的结果连接起来。结果通常被称为树形图上的"节点"。

这是抛两枚硬币的树形图和结果表：

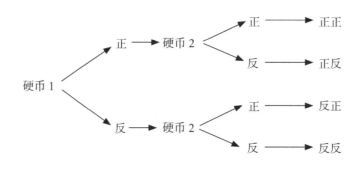

硬币 1	硬币 2	样本事件
正	正	正正
正	反	正反
反	正	反正
反	反	反反

树形图的另一个例子：假设当地冰激凌车中 30% 的单勺冰激凌以盒装形式出售，另外 70% 以甜筒装形式出售。还假设冰激凌车销售三种不同口味的冰激凌（巧克力、牛奶和草莓口味），并且单勺销售量的 50% 是巧克力

口味的，30% 是牛奶口味的，20% 是草莓口味的。树形图如下：

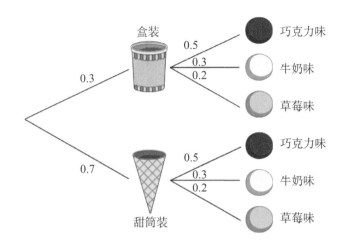

2.42　计数与乘法原理

通过乘法原理，将每个事件中的选项数量相乘来计算一系列事件中结果的数量。

$$n(a,b) = n(A)n(B)$$

要找出一组事件中结果的数量，可将这组事件中的每个事件的结果数量相乘。

例 1：

3 位数的密码组合可能有多少种结果？密码只能包含数字。

每位数字有 10 种可能，所以可能的结果数量为：

$$n = 10 \times 10 \times 10 = 1000 。$$

例 2：

加拿大的邮政编码可能有几个？

$$n(邮政编码) = 26 \times 10 \times 26 \times 10 \times 26 \times 10 = 17576000$$

2.43　独立事件和乘法原理

如果有两个事件 A 和 B，并且事件 B 发生的概率不受事件 A 发生的影

响，则 A 和 B 被认为是独立事件，那么

$$P(B|A) = P(B)。$$

这也可以用另一个交集公式来证明：

$$P(A \cap B) = P(A)P(B)。$$

例子：

一个袋子里有三个不同颜色的弹珠（红色、绿色、蓝色）。如果你从袋子里连续抽出两次绿色弹珠，并在每次抽取后将弹珠放回原处，证明这两次抽取是独立的。

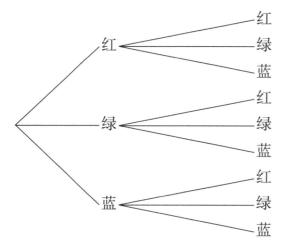

根据树形图，抽出两次绿色弹珠的概率是 1/9。如果我们使用交集公式，那么

$$P(\text{Green} \cap \text{Green}) = P(\text{Green})P(\text{Green}) = \frac{1}{3} \times \frac{1}{3} = \frac{1}{9}，$$

从而证明这两个事件是独立的。

—— Lesson 4 ——

Tree Diagram and Outcome Table

🍁 2.41　What Is a Tree Diagram?

A tree diagram is a way of visualizing all possible outcomes and probabilities for a given situation. Tree diagrams are also called decision trees, and they are useful in charting the possible outcomes of the dependent events. In a tree diagram, each "branch" of the tree connects an idea or a step in the process to a possible outcome. Outcomes are commonly referred to as "nodes" on a tree diagram.

Here is the tree diagram and outcome table of flipping two coins:

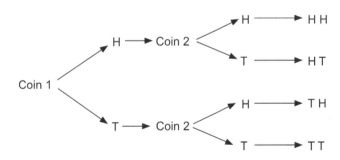

Coin 1	Coin 2	Sample Event
H	H	HH
H	T	HT
T	H	TH
T	T	TT

Here is another example of tree diagram: Suppose 30% of single-scoop ice cream from the local ice cream van is sold in a carton and the other 70% is sold in a cone. Suppose also that the ice cream van sells three different flavors of ice cream—chocolate, milk, and strawberry—and that 50% of single-scoop sales are chocolate, 30% are milk, and 20% are strawberry. The tree diagram is as follows:

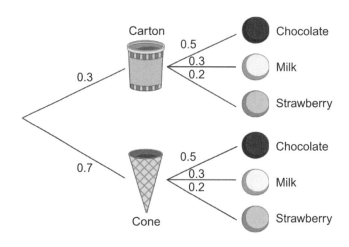

🍁 2.42 Counting and Multiplicative Principle

We can use the multiplicative principle for counting the number of outcomes within a series of events by multiplying the number of options in every event.

$$n(a,b)=n(A)n(B)$$

To find out the number of outcomes in a collection of events, we can multiply the outcome number in each event.

Example 1:

How many outcomes are possible with a 3-digit password combination? The password can only contain numbers.

Since there are 10 numbers available for each digit, the possible outcomes are:

$$n=10\times10\times10=1000.$$

Example 2:

How many postal codes are possible in Canada?

$$n(\text{postal code}) = 26 \times 10 \times 26 \times 10 \times 26 \times 10 = 17576000$$

🍁 2.43 Independent Events and Multiplicative Principle

If there are two events A and B, and the probability of occurrence of event B is not affected by the occurrence of event A, then A and B are considered independent events. Then,

$$P(B|A) = P(B).$$

This can also be proved by another formula of intersection:

$$P(A \cap B) = P(A)P(B).$$

Example:

A bag contains three different colored marbles (red, green, blue). If you draw the green marble from the bag twice in a row and put the marble back after each drawing, prove that the two drawings are independent.

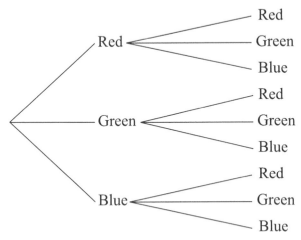

According to the tree diagram, the probability of drawing the green marble twice is 1/9. And if we use the formula of intersetion, then

$$P(\text{Green} \cap \text{Green}) = P(\text{Green})P(\text{Green}) = \frac{1}{3} \times \frac{1}{3} = \frac{1}{9},$$

which proves that the two events are independent.

—— 第 5 课 ——
排列

🍁 2.51　阶乘

阶乘是小于或等于给定正整数的所有正整数的乘积。当需要使用一系列连续数字的乘积时，我们可以使用阶乘表示法。这是一种更方便的方式。

$$n! = n \times (n-1) \times (n-2) \times \ldots \times 1$$

例子：

对 8 个不同的人进行排序，可以用多少种不同的方式？

$$8! = 8 \times 7 \times 6 \times 5 \times 4 \times 3 \times 2 \times 1 = 40320$$

🍁 2.52　排列

一个集合的排列方式的数量可以表示为 $_nP_n$ 或 $P(n, n)$，其中 n 表示集合中的元素数量。

例子：

将 6 只不同的狗排成一排，可以用多少种不同的方式？

$$_6P_6 = 6! = 720$$

在其他情况下，我们可能需要从集合中的 n 个元素中选择 r 个元素进行排列，可以写为：$_nP_r$ 或 $P(n, r)$。这可以表达为"如果需要排序的话，从集合中的 n 个元素中选择 r 个元素进行排列，有多少种不同的方式？"

$$_nP_r = \frac{n!}{(n-r)!}$$

例子：

一家公司想在全国范围内建立仓库网络。该公司将在 6 个可能的地点中选择 4 个地点。因为仓库将按顺序建立，所以需要排序。排列数为：

$$_6P_4 = \frac{6!}{(6-4)!} = 360 。$$

学生应注意问题中的"需要排序"。如果问题特别指出需要排序，那么我们应该计算排列的数量，否则我们应该计算组合的数量。

❧ 2.53　有重复元素的排列

如果需要排列的样本空间中存在非唯一元素怎么办？我们可以使用下面的公式来计算排列方式的数量：

$$N = \frac{n!}{a!} 。$$

N 表示排列方式的数量，n 表示样本空间中元素的数量，a 表示相同元素的数量。

例子：

"community"中的字母有多少种排列方式？

$$N = \frac{n!}{a!} = \frac{9!}{2!} = 181440$$

❧ 2.54　排列与概率

现在让我们看一个包含概率和排列的更复杂的问题。

例子：

袋子里有 8 个编号分别为 1—8 的球。你一个一个地抽取 4 个，抽取后不放回。抽中编号为 1—4 的球的概率是多少？

$P = \dfrac{事件空间}{样本空间}$，其中事件空间是抽中编号为 1—4 的球的方式的数量，样本空间是从 8 个球中抽取 4 个的方式的数量。

$$P = \frac{事件空间}{样本空间} = \frac{4!}{8!/(8-4)!} = \frac{24}{1680} \approx 0.0143 = 1.43\%$$

记住，当问题将概率与排列结合在一起时，学生应该清楚所使用的公式，并理解问题中的事件空间和样本空间分别指的是哪一部分。

— Lesson 5 —
Permutations

🍁 2.51   Factorials

A factorial is the product of all positive integers less than or equal to a given positive integer. When we need to use the product of a series of consecutive numbers, we can use factorial notation. It is a more convenient way.

$$n! = n \times (n-1) \times (n-2) \times \ldots \times 1$$

Example:

How many different ways can you sequence 8 different people?

$$8! = 8 \times 7 \times 6 \times 5 \times 4 \times 3 \times 2 \times 1 = 40320$$

🍁 2.52   Permutations

The number of ways a specific set can be arranged can be expressed as $_nP_n$ or $P(n, n)$, where n represents the number of items in the set.

Example:

How many different ways can we arrange 6 different dogs in a row?

$$_6P_6 = 6! = 720$$

In other circumstances, we may need to select r items out of n items in the set and arrange them, which can be written as: $_nP_r$ or $P(n, r)$. This can be expressed as "How many different ways can you arrange r items from a set of n items if order matters?"

$$_nP_r = \frac{n!}{(n-r)!}$$

Example:

A company wants to build out its warehouse network across the country. It will commit to 4 locations out of 6 possible sites. Order matters because they will be built sequentially. The number of permutations is:

$$_6P_4 = \frac{6!}{(6-4)!} = 360.$$

Students should pay attention to "order matters" in the question. If the question specially points out that order does matter, then we should calculate permutations, otherwise we should calculate combinations.

🍁 2.53　Permutations with Repeated Items

What if there are non-unique items in the sample space that we need to arrange? We can calculate the number of permutations using the formula:

$$N = \frac{n!}{a!}.$$

N represents the calculated permutations, n represents the number of items in the sample space, and a represents the number of items being identical.

Example:

How many ways can we arrange the letters in "community"?

$$N = \frac{n!}{a!} = \frac{9!}{2!} = 181440$$

🍁 2.54　Permutations and Probability

Now let's look at a more complex problem containing probabilities and permutations.

Example:

There are 8 balls numbered 1 – 8 respectively in a bag. You draw four balls one by one without replacement. What is the probability of drawing the balls numbered 1 – 4?

$P = \dfrac{\text{event space}}{\text{sample space}}$, where the event space is the number of ways of drawing 4 balls numbered 1 – 4, and the sample space is the number of ways of drawing 4 balls out of 8 balls.

$$P = \frac{\text{event space}}{\text{sample space}} = \frac{4!}{8!/(8-4)!} = \frac{24}{1680} \approx 0.0143 = 1.43\%$$

Remember, when the question combines probability with permutation, students should be clear about the formula being used, and understand which parts the event space and the sample space in the question refer to respectively.

组合

2.61 组合

计算组合的数量时，元素的顺序并不重要。

$$C(n,r) = {}_nC_r = \binom{n}{r} = \frac{n!}{(n-r)!\,r!}$$

学生可能会将组合与排列混淆。它们的不同之处在于，在组合中，不需要考虑排序，而在排列中，需要考虑排序。

例子：

假设我们要做一份包含三种不同水果的水果沙拉。选项包括香蕉、苹果、草莓、蓝莓、葡萄、橙子和梨。有多少种不同的结果？

在这种情况下，不需要考虑排序。无论先选择苹果还是先选择香蕉，结果都是相同的，因此用组合来计算。

$$C(7,3) = {}_7C_3 = \binom{7}{3} = \frac{7!}{(7-3)!\,3!} = 35$$

我们可以看到，如果不考虑排序，结果会少很多。

2.62 组合乘法

可以将一组组合相乘以确定结果的总数。

总结果 = n(组合 1) × n(组合 2) × ……

例子：

一个高中俱乐部由 4 名一年级学生、5 名二年级学生、5 名三年级学生和 6 名四年级学生组成。一个由 10 人组成的委员会，包括 2 名一年级学生、2 名二年级学生、3 名三年级学生和 3 名四年级学生，有多少种选择方式？

一年级学生的组合为 $C(4, 2)$，二年级学生的组合为 $C(5, 2)$，三年级学生的组合为 $C(5, 3)$，四年级学生的组合为 $C(6, 3)$。所以，

$$总数 = \frac{4!}{(4-2)!2!} \times \frac{5!}{(5-2)!2!} \times \frac{5!}{(5-3)!3!} \times \frac{6!}{(6-3)!3!} = 12000$$

2.63 组合和概率

有时我们在解决概率问题时，也会使用组合。

例子：

假设你有 10 颗弹珠：4 颗是蓝色的，6 颗是红色的。你随机抽出 3 颗弹珠。3 颗弹珠都是蓝色的概率是多少？

$$P(成功) = \frac{成功的方式的数量}{可能的结果的总数}$$

抽出 3 颗蓝色弹珠的方法有 $_4C_3$ 种。全部组合有 $_{10}C_3$ 种。

$$P(3颗弹珠都是蓝色的) = \frac{\binom{4}{3}}{\binom{10}{3}} = \frac{4}{120} = \frac{1}{30} \approx 3.33\%$$

抽出的 3 个弹珠都是蓝色的概率约为 3.33%。

Lesson 6
Combinations

🍁 2.61   Combinations

When the number of possible combinations is calculated, the order of the items does not matter.

$$C(n,r) = {}_nC_r = \binom{n}{r} = \frac{n!}{(n-r)!r!}$$

Students may confuse combination with permutation. The difference is that in combination, order DOES NOT matter, whereas in permutation, order DOES matter.

Example:

Let's say we are to make a fruit salad which contains three different kinds of fruit. The options are banana, apple, strawberry, blueberry, grape, orange and pear. How many different outcomes are there?

In this case, order is not important. It does not matter whether we pick apple or banana first, so the calculation involves combination.

$$C(7,3) = {}_7C_3 = \binom{7}{3} = \frac{7!}{(7-3)!3!} = 35$$

We can see that the result is much smaller if order is not important.

🍁 2.62   Combination Multiplication

A set of combinations can be multiplied together in order to determine the total number of outcomes.

$$\text{Total outcomes} = n(\text{combination 1}) \times n(\text{combination 2}) \times \ldots$$

Example:

A high school club consists of 4 freshmen, 5 sophomores, 5 juniors, and 6 seniors. How many ways can a committee of 10 people be chosen that includes 2 freshmen, 2 sophomores, 3 juniors and 3 seniors?

The combination for freshmen is C(4, 2), for sophomores is C(5, 2), for juniors is C(5, 3), for seniors is C(6, 3). Therefore,

$$\text{The total number} = \frac{4!}{(4-2)!2!} \times \frac{5!}{(5-2)!2!} \times \frac{5!}{(5-3)!3!} \times \frac{6!}{(6-3)!3!} = 12000$$

🍁 2.63   Combinations and Probability

Sometimes when we solve the probabilities problems, we also use combinations.

Example:

Suppose you have 10 marbles: 4 blue and 6 red. You choose 3 marbles without looking. What is the probability that all 3 marbles are blue?

$$P(\text{success}) = \frac{\text{number of ways to get success}}{\text{total number of possible outcomes}}$$

There are $_4C_3$ ways to choose the blue marbles. There are $_{10}C_3$ total combinations.

$$P(\text{all 3 marbles are blue}) = \frac{\binom{4}{3}}{\binom{10}{3}} = \frac{4}{120} = \frac{1}{30} \approx 3.33\%$$

There is approximately a 3.33% chance that all three marbles drawn are blue.

概率分布

Probability Distributions

对学生的期望

　　在本单元结束时，学生应该能够展示对离散概率分布的理解，用数字、图形和代数方式表示它们，确定期望值，并解决各种应用中的相关问题。学生还应该能够展示对连续概率分布的理解，与离散概率分布建立联系，确定标准差，描述正态分布的关键特征，并解决各种应用中的相关问题。[1]

Expectations for Students

At the end of this unit, students should demonstrate an understanding of discrete probability distributions, represent them numerically, graphically, and algebraically, determine expected values, and solve related problems from a variety of applications. Students should also demonstrate an understanding of continuous probability distributions, make connections to discrete probability distributions, determine standard deviations, describe key features of the normal distribution, and solve related problems from a variety of applications. [2]

---

[1][2] Ministry of Education of Ontario. *The Ontario Curriculum, Grades 11 and 12: Mathematics* [M/OL]. Toronto: Queen's Printer for Ontario, 2007: 111-122 [2024-04-29]. https://www.edu.gov.on.ca/eng/curriculum/secondary/math1112currb.pdf

— 第 1 课 —
概率分布

🍁 3.11　什么是概率分布？

概率分布是描述变量不同可能值的概率的数学函数。

🍁 3.12　理解离散随机变量的概率分布

变量是可以测量的特征。我们可以将变量描述为定量的或定性的。

离散随机变量是一种仅取有限个不同值的变量。

连续随机变量是仅具有连续值的随机变量。

例子：

掷骰子的概率分布（频率分布和图表）

	结果	概率
1	1	1/6
2	2	1/6
3	3	1/6
4	4	1/6
5	5	1/6
6	6	1/6

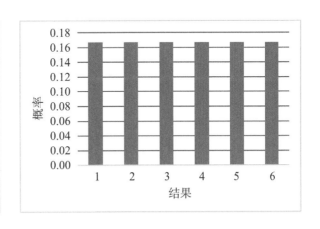

🍁 3.13　期望值

期望值是统计实验的所有可能结果以取得该结果的概率为权数的加权平

均数。期望值被定义为范围内值的加权平均数。期望值的公式如下：

$$E(X) = \sum_{i=1}^{n} x_i P(x_i) \text{。}$$

x_i 表示结果，$P(x_i)$ 表示该结果的概率。

例 1：

计算掷两个骰子的总和的期望值。

	1	2	3	4	5	6	7	8	9	10	11
总和	2	3	4	5	6	7	8	9	10	11	12
概率	1/36	2/36	3/36	4/36	5/36	6/36	5/36	4/36	3/36	2/36	1/36

注意，总和具有不同的概率。

$$E(X) = 2 \times \frac{1}{36} + 3 \times \frac{2}{36} + \ldots + 12 \times \frac{1}{36} = \frac{252}{36} = 7$$

例 2：

一个盒子里有 80 个球，其中 70 个是黑球，其余是白球。玩家必须支付 100 美元才能从盒子中随机挑选一个球。如果玩家拿到白球，他将赢得 750 美元。这个赌注的期望收益是多少？

得到黑球的概率为 70/80，得到白球的概率为 10/80。所以，

$$E(X) = -100 \times \frac{70}{80} + (750 - 100) \times \frac{10}{80} = -87.5 + 81.25 = -6.25 \text{。}$$

期望收益为 -6.25 美元。

— Lesson 1 —
Probability Distribution

🍁 3.11 What Is Probability Distribution?

A probability distribution is a mathematical function that describes the probability of different possible values of a variable.

🍁 3.12 Understanding Probability Distributions for Discrete Random Variables

A variable is a characteristic that can be measured. We can describe a variable as quantitative or qualitative.

A discrete random variable is one which may take on only a countable number of distinct values.

A continuous random variable is a random variable that has only continuous values.

Example:

Probability distribution of rolling a dice (frequency distribution and graph)

	Outcome	Probability
1	1	1/6
2	2	1/6
3	3	1/6
4	4	1/6
5	5	1/6
6	6	1/6

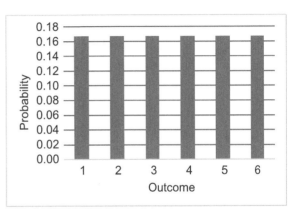

3.13　Expected Value

The expected value is the weighted average of all the possible outcomes of a statistical experiment, based on their probabilities. The expected value is defined as the weighted average of the values in the range. The expected value formula is as follows:

$$E(X) = \sum_{i=1}^{n} x_i P(x_i).$$

x_i represents an outcome, and $P(x_i)$ represents the probability of the outcome.

Example 1:

Calculate the expected value of the sum of rolling two dice.

	1	2	3	4	5	6	7	8	9	10	11
Sum	2	3	4	5	6	7	8	9	10	11	12
Probability	1/36	2/36	3/36	4/36	5/36	6/36	5/36	4/36	3/36	2/36	1/36

Note that the sums have different probabilities.

$$E(X) = 2 \times \frac{1}{36} + 3 \times \frac{2}{36} + \ldots + 12 \times \frac{1}{36} = \frac{252}{36} = 7$$

Example 2:

There are 80 balls in a box, of which 70 are black and the rest are white. A player has to pay $100 to pick a ball randomly from the box. If the player gets a white ball, he wins $750. What is the expected profit of this bet?

The probability of getting a black ball is 70/80, and the probability of getting a white ball is 10/80. Therefore,

$$E(X) = -100 \times \frac{70}{80} + (750 - 100) \times \frac{10}{80} = -87.5 + 81.25 = -6.25.$$

The expected value of profit gained is −6.25 dollars.

2

— 第 2 课 —

二项式定理和杨辉三角形

展开二项式时，二项式定理被认为非常有用。展开的模式与杨辉三角形一致。杨辉三角形是数字的三角形排列，它给出二项式展开式的系数。

当项 $(a+b)$ 在不同条件下展开时，

$$(a+b)^0 = 1 \text{,}$$

$$(a+b)^1 = a+b \text{,}$$

$$(a+b)^2 = a^2 + 2ab + b^2 \text{,}$$

$$(a+b)^3 = a^3 + 3a^2b + 3ab^2 + b^3 \text{,}$$

$$(a+b)^4 = a^4 + 4a^3b + 6a^2b^2 + 4ab^3 + b^4 \text{。}$$

从上面的结果可以总结出，第一个变量的指数是递减的，第二个变量的指数是递增的。可以通过组合来确定系数。所以，

$$(a+b)^n = \binom{n}{0}a^n + \binom{n}{1}a^{n-1}b + \binom{n}{2}a^{n-2}b^2 + \ldots + \binom{n}{r}a^{n-r}b^r + \ldots + \binom{n}{n}b^n \text{。}$$

$(a+b)^n$ 的展开式的第 $r+1$ 项是 $T_{r+1} = \binom{n}{r}a^{n-r}b^r$。

例 1：

写出 $(a+b)^5$ 的展开式。

$$(a+b)^5 = \binom{5}{0}a^{5-0} + \binom{5}{1}a^{5-1}b + \binom{5}{2}a^{5-2}b^2 + \binom{5}{3}a^{5-3}b^3 + \binom{5}{4}a^{5-4}b^4 + \binom{5}{5}b^5$$

$$= a^5 + 5a^4b + 10a^3b^2 + 10a^2b^3 + 5ab^4 + b^5$$

例 2：

求 $(y-2x)^6$ 的展开式的第二项。

根据

$$T_{r+1} = \binom{n}{r} a^{n-r} b^r,$$

$$T_{1+1} = \binom{6}{1} y^{6-1} (-2x)^1 = -12y^5 x。$$

注意，展开式的第二项表示 r 等于 1，而不是 2，并且二项式的底数中的第二项是 $-2x$，而不是 $2x$。这是解决此类问题的关键。学生需要多练习，熟能生巧。

— Lesson 2 —

Binomial Theorem and Pascal's Triangle

The binomial theorem is considered very useful when a binomial expression is being expanded. The pattern of expansion corresponds to Pascal's triangle. Pascal's triangle is the triangular arrangement of numbers that gives the coefficients in the expansion of any binomial expression.

When the term ($a + b$) is expanded under different conditions,

$$(a+b)^0 = 1,$$

$$(a+b)^1 = a+b,$$

$$(a+b)^2 = a^2 + 2ab + b^2,$$

$$(a+b)^3 = a^3 + 3a^2b + 3ab^2 + b^3,$$

$$(a+b)^4 = a^4 + 4a^3b + 6a^2b^2 + 4ab^3 + b^4.$$

From the result above, it can be concluded that the exponent of the first variable is descending and the exponent of the second variable is ascending. The coefficients can be determined by applying combinations. Therefore,

$$(a+b)^n = \binom{n}{0}a^n + \binom{n}{1}a^{n-1}b + \binom{n}{2}a^{n-2}b^2 + \ldots + \binom{n}{r}a^{n-r}b^r + \ldots + \binom{n}{n}b^n.$$

The $(r+1)$th term of the expansion of $(a+b)^n$ is $T_{r+1} = \binom{n}{r}a^{n-r}b^r$.

Example 1:

Write the expansion of $(a+b)^5$.

$$(a+b)^5 = \binom{5}{0}a^{5-0} + \binom{5}{1}a^{5-1}b + \binom{5}{2}a^{5-2}b^2 + \binom{5}{3}a^{5-3}b^3 + \binom{5}{4}a^{5-4}b^4 + \binom{5}{5}b^5$$

$$= a^5 + 5a^4b + 10a^3b^2 + 10a^2b^3 + 5ab^4 + b^5$$

Example 2:

Find the second term of the expansion of $(y-2x)^6$.

According to

$$T_{r+1} = \binom{n}{r}a^{n-r}b^r,$$

$$T_{1+1} = \binom{6}{1}y^{6-1}(-2x)^1 = -12y^5x.$$

Note that the second term of the expansion indicates that r is equal to 1, not 2, and that the second term of the base of the binomial is $-2x$ instead of 2x. They are the key points to solve this kind of problem. Students will need to practice more for perfection.

— 第 3 课 —

二项式概率分布

🍁 3.31　什么是二项式实验？

如果一个实验有固定数量 (n) 的独立试验，并且只有两种可能的结果，则可以将其视为二项式实验。结果可以描述为成功或失败。对于概率计算，成功的概率定义为 p，而失败的概率为 $1-p$。

🍁 3.32　二项式随机变量

二项式随机变量是离散随机变量的一种特殊类型。它是一定次数 (n) 的试验中成功的次数，通常称为 X，因此失败的次数通常表示为 $n-X$。该二项式随机变量 (X) 的概率分布称为二项式分布。

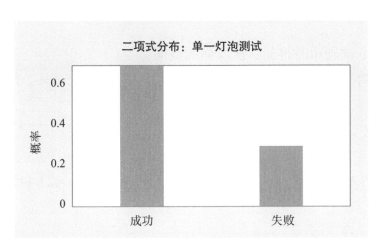

在单个事件的二项式分布中，$n = 1$。根据上图，成功的概率为 70%。

注意，二项式实验可以重复进行一定次数 (n) 的试验。

抛硬币是一个二项式实验。接下来我们看一下 $n = 10$，换句话说，一枚硬币被抛了 10 次时的二项式分布。

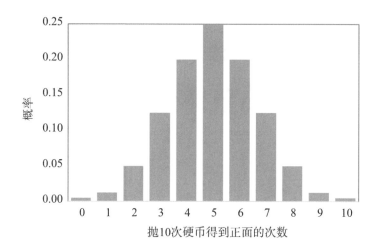

抛10次硬币得到正面的次数

🍁 3.33 二项式概率

可用于计算二项式概率的公式：

$$P\left(X=k\right)=\binom{n}{k}p^{k}\left(1-p\right)^{n-k}。$$

P 代表我们需要计算的概率，k 是成功的次数，n 是试验总次数，p 是单次试验成功的概率。

例子：

计算抛 6 次硬币时得到 2 次反面的概率。

让我们将反面视为成功，正面视为失败，则 $p=1/2$，$k=2$ 且 $n=6$。

$$P\left(X=k\right)=\binom{n}{k}p^{k}\left(1-p\right)^{n-k}$$

$$P\left(X=2\right)=\binom{6}{2}\left(\frac{1}{2}\right)^{2}\left(1-\frac{1}{2}\right)^{6-2}=15\times\frac{1}{4}\times\frac{1}{16}=\frac{15}{64}\approx23.44\%$$

🍁 3.34 二项式概率分布

接下来我们可以使用分布图来验证我们的计算。

例子：

确定如果我们抛 5 次硬币，得到至少 3 次正面的概率。

$$P(X \geq 3) = P(X = 3) + P(X = 4) + P(X = 5) = \frac{5}{16} + \frac{5}{32} + \frac{1}{32} = \frac{1}{2}$$

结果与二项式分布条形图相符。

$$0.3125 + 0.15625 + 0.03125 = 0.5$$

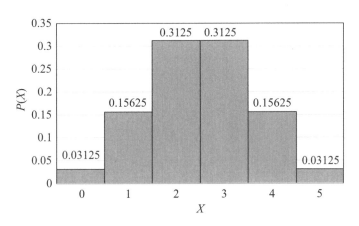

🍁 3.35 二项式实验的期望值

二项式实验的期望值可以用以下公式计算：

$$E(X) = np,$$

其中 n 是试验次数，p 是成功概率。

这部分内容与前面的期望值的内容相关。

下面的例子包括概率和期望值：

一个盒子里面有 10 颗不同颜色的糖果。一颗糖果是红色的概率为 25%。

1）一个盒子里正好有 4 颗红色糖果的概率是多少？

这可以被视为二项式实验，因为只有两种结果：红色和非红色。

已知 $n = 10$，$p = 0.25$，$X = 4$，所以：

$$P(X = 4) = \binom{10}{4} 0.25^4 (1 - 0.25)^{10-4} \approx 14.6\% \text{。}$$

2）如果我们打开 4 个盒子，预计有多少颗糖果是红色的？

因为 1 盒中有 10 颗糖果，所以我们总共有 40 颗糖果。那么 n 是 40。一颗糖果为红色的概率是 25%，那么 p 是 0.25。我们将这两个数字相乘得出期望值。

$$E(X) = np = 40 \times 0.25 = 10$$

— Lesson 3 —
Binomial Probability Distribution

🍁 3.31　What Is a Binomial Experiment?

If an experiment has a fixed number (n) of independent trials, and there are only two possible outcomes, it can be considered as a binomial experiment. The outcomes can be described as either success or failure. For calculations of probability, the probability of success is defined as p, whereas the probability of failure is $1-p$.

🍁 3.32　Binomial Random Variable

A binomial random variable is a particular type of discrete random variable. It is the number of successes within a fixed number (n) of trials, often called X, so the number of failures is usually represented as $n-X$. The probability distribution of this binomial random variable (X) is called a binomial distribution.

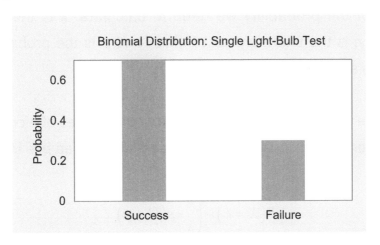

For a binomial distribution of a single event, $n = 1$. Based on the graph above, the probability of success is 70%.

Be aware that the binomial experiment can be repeated for a fixed number (n) of trials.

Tossing a coin is a binomial experiment. Next let's look at a binomial distribution of $n = 10$, in other words, when a coin is flipped 10 times.

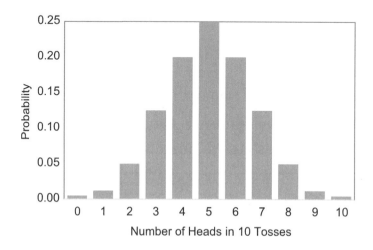

🍁 3.33 Binomial Probability

The formula that can be used to calculate binomial probabilities:

$$P(X = k) = \binom{n}{k} p^k (1-p)^{n-k}.$$

P stands for the probability we need to calculate, k is the number of successes, n is the total number of trials, and p is the probability of the success in a single trial.

Example:

Calculate the probability of gaining 2 tails out of 6 tosses of a coin.

Let's consider tails as success and heads as failure, then $p = 1/2$, $k = 2$ and $n = 6$.

$$P(X = k) = \binom{n}{k} p^k (1-p)^{n-k}$$

$$P(X=2)=\binom{6}{2}\left(\frac{1}{2}\right)^{2}\left(1-\frac{1}{2}\right)^{6-2}=15\times\frac{1}{4}\times\frac{1}{16}=\frac{15}{64}\approx 23.44\%$$

🍁 3.34　Binomial Probability Distribution

Next we can use distribution graph to verify our calculation.

Example:

Determine the probability of getting at least 3 heads if we toss a coin 5 times.

$$P(X\geqslant 3)=P(X=3)+P(X=4)+P(X=5)=\frac{5}{16}+\frac{5}{32}+\frac{1}{32}=\frac{1}{2}$$

The result corresponds to the binomial distribution bar chart.

$$0.3125 + 0.15625 + 0.03125 = 0.5$$

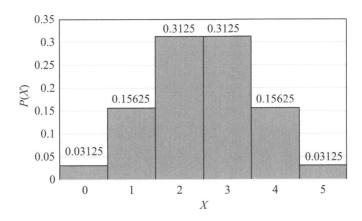

🍁 3.35　Expected Value in a Binomial Experiment

The expected value of a binomial experiment can be computed with the formula:

$$E(X)=np,$$

where n is the number of trials, and p is the probability of success.

This part relates to the previous content of expected value.

The following example includes probability and expected value:

A box contains 10 candies of different colors. There is a 25% chance that a candy is red.

1) What is the probability that exactly 4 candies in a box are red?

This can be considered as a binomial experiment since there are only two outcomes: red and not red.

We have that $n = 10$, $p = 0.25$, $X = 4$, so:

$$P(X=4)=\binom{10}{4}0.25^4(1-0.25)^{10-4}\approx 14.6\%.$$

2) If we open up 4 boxes, how many candies are expected to be red?

Since there are 10 candies in 1 box, we have 40 candies in total. Therefore n is 40. The chance for a candy to be red is 25%, so p is 0.25. Then we multiply the two numbers together to get the expected value.

$$E(X)=np=40\times 0.25=10$$

━━ 第 4 课 ━━
理解连续随机变量的概率分布

🍁 3.41　二项式分布与正态分布的关系

　　有时二项式实验的试验次数可能非常多，如果我们继续使用二项式概率来解决这个问题，计算可能会变得非常复杂。因此，我们可以使用正态分布来更简单地解决问题。也就是说，我们可以应用与解决正态分布问题相同的方法。例如，使用平均数、标准差、z 分数及 z 表。

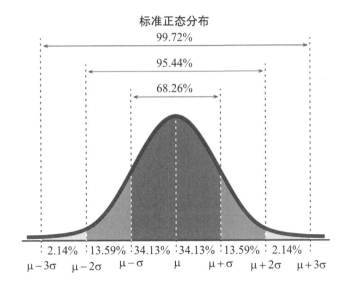

标准正态分布
99.72%
95.44%
68.26%

| 2.14% | 13.59% | 34.13% | 34.13% | 13.59% | 2.14% |

$\mu-3\sigma$　$\mu-2\sigma$　$\mu-\sigma$　μ　$\mu+\sigma$　$\mu+2\sigma$　$\mu+3\sigma$

🍁 3.42　何时用正态分布估算二项式分布？

　　我们如何确保特定的二项式分布与正态分布曲线的模式相匹配？我们可以通过测试两个表达式来验证这一点：

$$np > 5 \text{ 且 } n(1-p) > 5,$$

其中 n 是试验总次数，p 是成功概率。

注意，我们必须确保两个计算都是正确的，其中只有一个正确则不允许我们使用正态曲线。

3.43 二项式分布的平均数和标准差

学生需要记住两个公式：

对于平均数，$\mu = np$；对于标准差，$\sigma = \sqrt{np(1-p)}$。

学生应该意识到与确定连续频率分布相关的挑战，例如，无法获得变量的所有值。造成这种混乱的原因是变量的差异。当使用正态分布估算二项式概率时，我们假设变量是连续变量，而不是离散变量。解决这个问题的方法是在实际计算中使用连续性校正因子。我们可以把离散的 x 数值加上或减去 0.5。

例子：

62% 的 12 年级学生在某个城市学区上学。如果选择 500 名 12 年级儿童作为样本，求至少 290 名实际入学的概率。

首先，我们证明能用正态近似来解决这个二项式分布问题。

$n = 500$，$p = 62\%$，$1 - p = 38\%$，那么 $np = 310 > 5$ 且 $n(1-p) = 190 > 5$

然后，求平均数和标准差。

$$\mu = np = 310，\quad \sigma = \sqrt{np(1-p)} \approx 10.85$$

问题指出我们需要"求至少 290 名实际入学的概率"，即 $P(X \geqslant 290)$。使用连续性校正因子重写问题：$P(X \geqslant 290 - 0.5) = P(X \geqslant 289.5)$。

求 z 分数。

$$z = \frac{289.5 - 310}{10.85} \approx -1.89$$

使用 z 表查得概率为 97.06%。

— Lesson 4 —
Understanding Probability Distributions for Continuous Random Variables

🍁 3.41 Connection between Binomial Distribution and Normal Distribution

Sometimes the number of trials of binomial experiment can be very large, and if we continue to use binomial probability for this problem, the calculation may become very complicated. Hence we could use normal distribution to solve the question in an easier way. That is to say, we can apply the same method being used for normal distribution. For example, use the mean, standard deviation, z-score, and z-table.

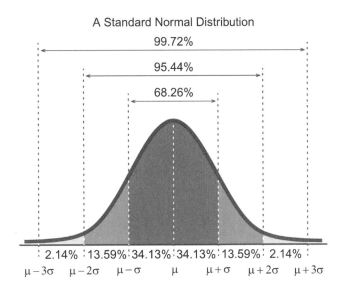

A Standard Normal Distribution

🍁 3.42　When to Use the Normal Distribution to Approximate the Binomial Distribution?

How can we make sure that a specific binomial distribution matches the pattern of a normal distribution curve? We can verify this by testing two expressions:

$$np > 5 \text{ and } n(1-p) > 5,$$

where *n* is the total number of trials and *p* is the probability of success.

Note that we must make sure that BOTH calculations are true, and that either one of them is correct does not allow us to use the normal curve.

🍁 3.43　Mean and Standard Deviation for Binomial Distribution

Students need to remember two formulas:

for the mean, $\mu = np$; for the standard deviation, $\sigma = \sqrt{np(1-p)}$.

Student should be aware of the challenges associated with determining a continuous frequency distribution, for example, the inability to capture all values of the variable. The reason of this confusion is the difference of the variables. When using normal distribution to approximate binomial probabilities, we assume the variables are continuous variables, not discrete variables. The solution to resolve this is using the continuity correction factor. We can add 0.5 or –0.5 to the discrete *x*-value.

Example:

62% of 12th graders attend school in a particular urban school district. If a sample of 500 12th grade children is selected, find the probability that at least 290 are actually enrolled in school.

First, we verify that we can use the normal approximation to the binomial distribution.

$n = 500, p = 62\%, 1-p = 38\%,$ so $np = 310 > 5$ and $n(1-p) = 190 > 5$

Then, find the mean and standard deviation.

$$\mu = np = 310, \ \sigma = \sqrt{np(1-p)} \approx 10.85$$

The question stated that we need to "find the probability that at least 290 are actually enrolled in school," i.e. $P(X \geqslant 290)$. Rewrite the problem using the continuity correction factor: $P(X \geqslant 290-0.5) = P(X \geqslant 289.5)$.

Find the z-score.

$$z = \frac{289.5 - 310}{10.85} \approx -1.89$$

Use the z-table to find the probability which is 97.06%.

OSSD

MDM4U

第4单元

数据组织

Unit 4

Data Organization

对学生的期望

在本单元结束时，学生应该能够了解数据在统计研究中的作用及数据固有的可变性，并区分不同类型的数据。学生应该能够描述理想样本的特征、一些抽样技术及原始数据收集的原则，并能收集和组织数据以解决问题。[1]

Expectations for Students

By the end of this unit, students should demonstrate an understanding of the role of data in statistical studies and the variability inherent in data, and distinguish different types of data. Students should be able to describe the characteristics of a good sample, some sampling techniques, and principles of primary data collection, and collect and organize data to solve a problem.[2]

---

[1][2] Ministry of Education of Ontario. *The Ontario Curriculum, Grades 11 and 12: Mathematics* [M/OL]. Toronto: Queen's Printer for Ontario, 2007: 111-122 [2024-04-29]. https://www.edu.gov.on.ca/eng/curriculum/secondary/math1112currb.pdf

第 1 课

理解数据概念

🍁 4.11 数据类型

数据是我们用作推理、讨论和计算基础的信息集合。我们可以将数据分为两类：定量数据和定性数据。定量数据是可以用数值来计数或测量的数据。定量数据的两种主要类型是离散数据和连续数据。离散数据是一些特定的值，这些值不能再细分，例如学生的数量或者硬币的数量。连续数据是一些可以分割成更小部分的值，例如体重或身高。定性数据是无法计数、测量或很难用数字表达的信息。定性数据用来描述质量或特征。

🍁 4.12 数据的不同显示方式

频率表显示一组值并为每个值分配一个频率。它有两列或三列。第一列将所有结果作为单独值或以组距的形式显示。第二列包括每个结果的计数符号，它也用线条告诉我们频率。它是可选的。第三列告诉我们每个结果的频率。

得分	计数符号	频率
4	II	2
5	II	2
6	IIII	4
7	₩	5
8	IIII	4
9	II	2
10	I	1

柱状图（也称条形图）使用宽度相同而高度／长度不同的条形对数据进行图形显示。一个条形与另一个条形之间的距离应始终一致。它可以是水平的或垂直的。每个条形的高度或长度与其值直接相关。

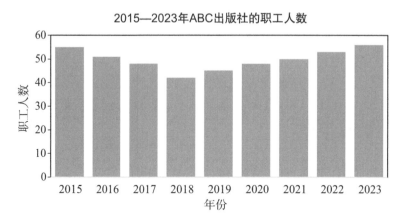

直方图是一种统计图，通过绘制的条形表示连续数据集的分布，每个条形代表特定的类别或组距。直方图看起来像条形图，但将连续度量的值分到不同的范围或矩形条中。

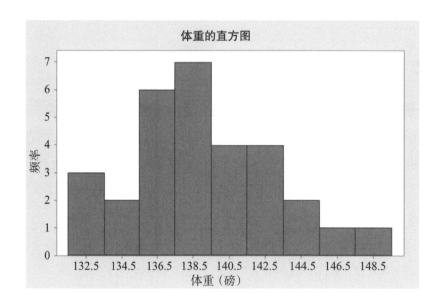

象形图画是一种使用图像来表示数据的方式。象形图画中的每个图像都代表一定数量的事物。

最喜欢的水果

水果	票数
🍎	☺☺☺☺☺☺☺☺☺☺
🍐	☺☺☺☺☺☺☺☺
🍇	☺☺
🍌	☺☺☺☺☺☺

1 票 = ☺

茎叶图将每个数据分为"叶"（通常是最后一位数字）和"茎"（前导数字）来显示数值数据。

电话通话时长

茎	叶
0	2 3 5 6
1	0 4 9
2	3 3
3	0 6
4	
6	6

示例：1|4 = 14 分钟

圆形图（也称饼状图）是数据的直观表示。在绘制圆形图时，将圆形划分为多个扇区，每个扇区代表整体的一部分。

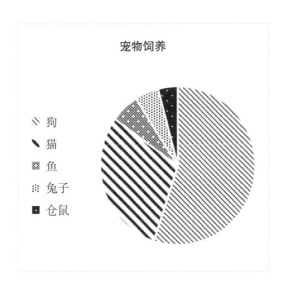

Understanding Data Concepts

🍁 4.11　Types of Data

Data is a collection of information that we use as a basis for reasoning, discussion and calculation. We can classify data into two categories: quantitative data and qualitative data. Quantitative data is the data that can be counted or measured in numerical values. The two main types of quantitative data are discrete data and continuous data. Discrete data are specific values that cannot be divided, such as the number of students or coins. Continuous data are values that can be split into smaller parts, such as weight or height. Qualitative data is information that cannot be counted, measured or easily expressed using numbers. Qualitative data are used to describe qualities or characteristics.

🍁 4.12　Different Ways of Displaying Data

A frequency table shows a set of values and assigns a frequency to each of them. It has two or three columns. The first column has all the outcomes as individual values or in the form of class intervals. The second column includes tally marks of each outcome, which also tells us about the frequency using lines. It is optional. The third column tells us about the frequency of each outcome.

Score	Tally Marks	Frequency
4	II	2
5	II	2
6	IIII	4
7	ꟷHꟷ	5
8	IIII	4
9	II	2
10	I	1

A bar graph (also called bar chart) is a graphical display of data using bars of equal width and different heights/lengths. The gap between one bar and another should be uniform throughout. It can be either horizontal or vertical. The height or length of each bar relates directly to its value.

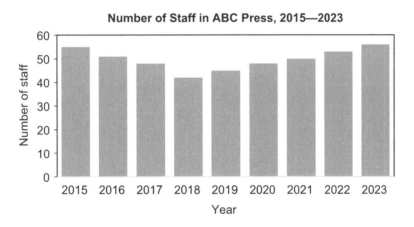

A histogram is a statistical graph that represents the distribution of a continuous data set through plotted bars, each representing a particular category or class interval. A histogram looks like a bar chart but groups values for a continuous measure into ranges, or bins.

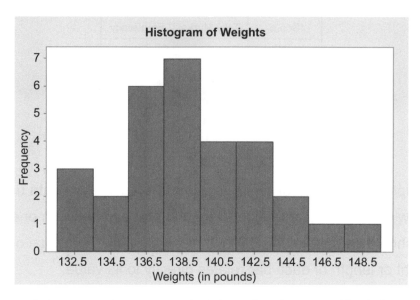

A pictograph is a way to represent data using images. Each image in the pictograph stands for a certain number of things.

Favorite Fruit

Fruit	Votes
🍎	☺☺☺☺☺☺☺☺☺☺
🍐	☺☺☺☺☺☺☺
🍇	☺☺
🍌	☺☺☺☺☺☺

1 vote = ☺

A stem-and-leaf plot displays numerical data by splitting each data point into a "leaf" (usually the last digit) and a "stem" (the leading digit or digits).

Phone Call Lengths

Stem	Leaf
0	2 3 5 6
1	0 4 9
2	3 3
3	0 6
4	
6	6

Key: 1|4 = 14 minutes

A circle graph (also called pie chart) is a visual representation of data, made by dividing a circle into sectors, each representing a part of the whole.

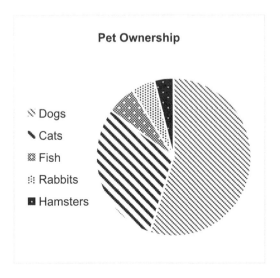

── 第 2 课 ──
变量及其表示

🍁 4.21　变量

变量是代表数值或数字的字母字符。在数学方程中，变量可以是任何字母，"x" 是最常用的。

在本课程中，变量可以被测量，也可以取不同值。

变量可以是定性的，也可以是定量的。定量变量包括离散变量和连续变量。

变量还可以分为自变量和因变量。自变量是因，因变量是果。换句话说，因变量取决于自变量的变化。

通常在统计图中，自变量位于横轴上，而因变量位于纵轴上。

🍁 4.22　用于表示变量的图表

散点图是表达两个变量之间关系的图表。它使研究人员能够直接了解数据的关系或趋势。通过散点图，考虑变量之间的关系，可以绘制一条最佳拟合线以便更好地理解。这条线是直线并把线与数据点之间的距离最小化。在线上方和下方有几乎相同数量的点。它可以用作预测工具。

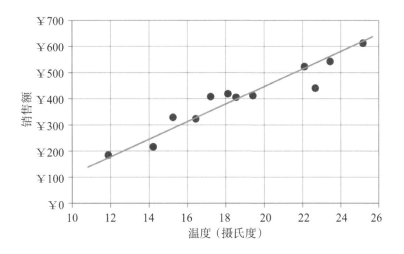

4.23 线性相关

线性相关度量的是两个随机变量之间的依赖程度。我们可以根据两个不同的标准来描述相关性。这两个标准是最佳拟合线的斜率以及从该线到散点图中的点的距离。因此，它可以分为正相关或负相关、强相关或弱相关。

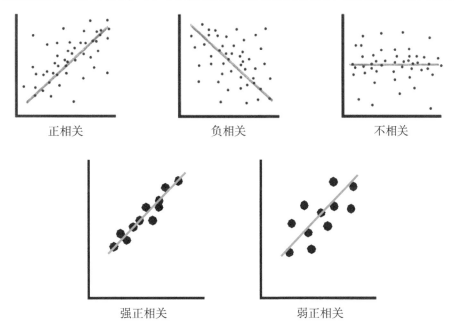

学生应该区分相关性之间的差异并正确标记它们。

—— Lesson 2 ——

Variables and Their Representation

🍁 4.21 Variables

A variable is defined as the alphabetic character that represents a numerical value or a number. In mathematical equations, variables can be any letter, and "x" is most commonly used.

In this course, a variable is a characteristic that can be measured and that can assume different values.

Variables can be qualitative and quantitative. Quantitative variables include discrete variables and continuous variables.

Variables can also be categorized as independent variables or dependent variables. Independent variables are the cause while dependent variables are the effect. In other words, dependent variables are dependent on the changes of independent variables.

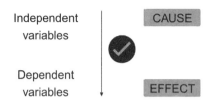

Normally in a statistical graph, the independent variable is on the horizontal axis while the dependent variable is on the vertical axis.

4.22　Graphs Used to Represent Variables

A scatter plot is a chart that expresses the relationship between two variables. It allows researchers to understand the relationship or trend of the data immediately. With the scatter plot, considering the relationship between the variables, a line of best fit could be drawn for better understanding. This line is straight and minimizes the distances between the line and the data points. There should be about an equal number of points above and below the line. It can be used as a prediction tool.

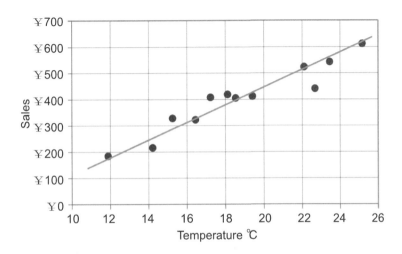

4.23　Linear Correlations

Linear correlation is a measure of dependence between two random variables. We can describe the correlation based on two different measures. The two measures are the slope of the line of best fit, and the distances from the line to the points in the scatter plot. Therefore, it can be classified as positive or negative correlation, and strong or weak correlation.

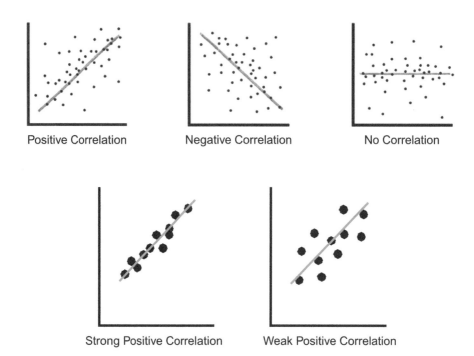

Positive Correlation   Negative Correlation   No Correlation

Strong Positive Correlation   Weak Positive Correlation

Students are expected to distinguish the differences between the correlations and label them correctly.

— 第 3 课 —
提出研究问题并根据数据得出结论

🍁 4.31 提出研究问题

thesis 这个单词的含义是体现原创性研究成果，特别是证实某一特定观点的论文。在数据管理中，是指研究人员希望回答或解决的问题。

选择研究问题时，我们应该能够陈述一个具体的问题，识别变量，可靠地测量变量，获得足够的数据来表述分析和处理这个问题。

我们还可以做出假设，预测变量之间的关系。

学生应能够根据数据的特点提出合理的研究问题。

🍁 4.32 得出结论

如果我们想从数据中得出结论，需要满足一些条件：

1）数据应该反映整体情况。

2）样本量要适合得出可靠的结论。

3）数据应反映问题的设计。

注意，有时相关性并不表示因果关系。学生应该认识到，即使两个变量之间存在关系，也不意味着一个变量是另一个变量的原因。

— Lesson 3 —

Developing a Thesis and Drawing Conclusions from Data

4.31 Developing a Thesis

The meaning of thesis is a dissertation embodying results of original research and especially substantiating a specific view. In data management, this refers to a question that researchers hope to answer or address.

When we choose a thesis, we should be able to state a specific question, identify the variables, measure the variables reliably, obtain enough data to formulate analysis and manage the topic.

We can also make a hypothesis, which is a prediction of the relationship between the variables.

Students should be able to raise a reasonable thesis based on the characteristics of data.

4.32 Drawing Conclusions

Some conditions need to be satisfied if we want to draw conclusions from data:

1) The data should represent the whole population.

2) The sample size should be fit for a reliable conclusion.

3) The data should reflect the design of the question.

Note that sometimes correlation does not indicate causation. Students should realize that even if there is a relationship between two variables, it does not mean that one variable is the cause of another one.

— 第 4 课 —
数据的时间范围和力量

4.41 数据的时间范围

在前几课中，我们已经介绍了数据分类的不同方式。此外，还可以使用时间范围来区分数据。这两种是瞬时数据和时间序列数据。

瞬时数据是针对大范围的个体收集的，用于描述某一时刻的情况。涉及这种数据的研究是横断面研究，通常在很短的时间内进行。

时间序列数据是在较长时间内收集的，侧重于较小的样本量。涉及这种数据的研究是纵向研究，经常会花费很长一段时间。

4.42 数据的力量

在媒体使用方面，数据呈现可能具有非常强大的影响力。我们应该意识到，有些数据可能会以误导性的方式展示，每个人都应该知道如何识别它们。

数据可能通过以下方式进行更改：

1）缩放不当

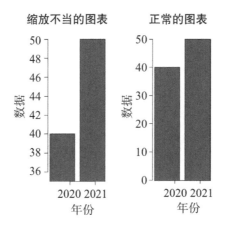

2）省略数据

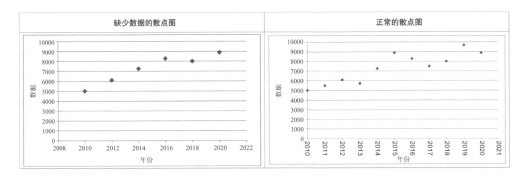

3）使用不同的视角

尽管具有相同的值，但由于透视原因，前面的柱子看起来比后面的柱子大。

4）以多种方式改变调查

例如，我们想要进行一项关于人们对快餐态度的调查，然后决定在麦当劳门口进行采访。

— Lesson 4 —

The Time Frame and Power of Data

🍁 4.41　The Time Frame of Data

In previous lessons, we have introduced different ways of data classification, and we can also use the time frame to differentiate data. Those two kinds are instantaneous data and time series data.

Instantaneous data are collected on a wide range of individuals to describe the situation at a certain moment. The study that involves this kind of data is cross-sectional study, usually conducted within a very short period of time.

Collected over an extended period of time, time series data focus on a smaller sample size. The study associated with this kind of data is longitudinal study, often taking up a very long period of time.

🍁 4.42　The Power of Data

Data presentation can be very powerful in terms of media use. We should be aware that some data could be demonstrated in a misleading way and everyone should know how to identify them.

Data could be altered using the following ways:

1) Improper Scaling

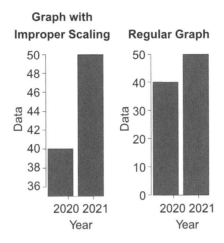

2) Omitting Data

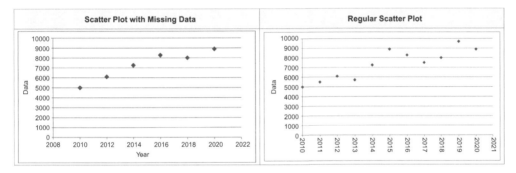

3) Using Different Viewing Angles

The column in the front appears larger than the column in the back due to perspective, despite having the same value.

4) Altering the Survey in Multiple Ways

For example, we want to conduct a survey about people's attitude toward fast food and we decide to carry out an interview in front of MacDonald's.

— 第 5 课 —
收集和准备数据

🍁 4.51 采集样本

在进行研究时，如果总体规模很大，则收集数据的最有利方法是抽样，这比从整体中获取数据速度更快、成本更低。研究的准确性取决于样本的选择。

🍁 4.52 抽样方法

所有的抽样类型都属于以下两个基本类别之一——

概率抽样： 研究人员可以计算出总体中任何一个个体被选中进行研究的概率。

非概率抽样： 研究人员无法计算总体中个体参与研究的概率。

概率抽样有四种类型——

简单随机抽样（SRS）： 研究人员不带任何偏见地随机从总体中抽取样本。当每个个体被选择参加研究的概率相同时，就会发生简单随机抽样。以抽签方式为例，所有受访者被选中的机会相同。

分层抽样： 研究人员将总体分为不同的组或层，然后在每层中进行随机抽样。例如，如果总体由 630 名女性和 370 名男性组成，你可以将总体分为男性和女性。然后，你可以通过简单随机抽样的方式选择 63 名女性受访者和 37 名男性受访者，以获得 100 名参与者的代表性样本。

系统抽样： 研究人员从一个随机的点开始按固定间隔选择个体作为研究参与者。例如，为了得到一个 25 人的样本，你可以把一个 250 人的总体分为 25 组，并使用每组中的第 5 个人作为研究参与者。

整群抽样： 研究人员将特定总体划分为组或群，然后随机选取几个群进行调查。例如，调查某个州居民的饮食习惯时，你可以根据这些居民居住的县将这些居民分成不同的群，然后使用简单随机抽样方法选择 8 个县进行研究。多阶段抽样（又称多阶段整群抽样）是一种更复杂的整群抽样。在多阶段抽样中，你在每个阶段使用越来越小的群体从总体中抽取样本。例如，这种方法常用于在全国调查中从分布广泛的大型人群中收集数据。

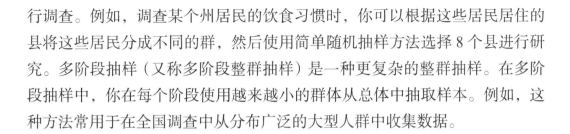 4.53　数据来源

如果数据是研究人员自己收集的，并且是直接分析的，那么这些数据是原始资料。

二手资料的数据不是研究人员自己收集的。

4.54　二手数据的优点和局限性

虽然原始资料是我们的最佳选择，但考虑到与研究相关的时间和成本，我们经常使用二手资料。

二手数据的优点：

1）与原始数据相比，二手数据为我们的项目提供了一种高效且易于获取的信息来源，节省了时间和成本。

2）利用现有的数据库，我们可以访问原本无法自己收集的数据。

3）从可靠来源获取的二手数据有时比我们自己收集的数据更可靠。

二手数据的局限性：

1）由于对数据不熟悉，我们需要更多时间来理解。

2）别人收集的数据对于解决我们项目中的问题可能不理想。

3）某些来源的数据质量可能无法保证。

4）二手资料可能缺乏关键变量。

4.55　准备数据

我们可以使用不同的软件程序来处理数据，例如 Excel、Apache 和 LibreOffice。

5

—— Lesson 5 ——
Collecting and Preparing Data

🍁 4.51   Collecting Samples

When conducting a research and the population size is large, the most beneficial way of collecting data is sampling, which is faster and less expensive than taking data from the entire population. The accuracy of the research relies on the sample selection.

🍁 4.52   Sampling Methods

All types of sampling fall into one of these two fundamental categories—
Probability Sampling: Researchers can calculate the probability of any single individual in the population being selected for the study.

Non-probability Sampling: Researchers cannot calculate the probability of being in the study for individuals within the population.

There are four types of probability sampling—

Simple Random Sampling (SRS): Researchers draw samples from a population by chance without any bias. Simple random sampling occurs when each individual has the same probability of being chosen for the study. Take, for example, the lottery method, in which all respondents have the same chance of being selected.

Stratified Sampling: Researchers divide the population into distinct groups, or strata, and select a random sample from each stratum. For example, if a population consists of 630 females and 370 males, you may divide the population into males and females. Then, you can choose 63 female respondents and 37 male respondents via simple random sampling to get a representative sample of 100 participants.

Systematic Sampling: Researchers select individuals at regular intervals from a random point as study participants. For example, in order to get a sample of 25 people, you can divide a population of 250 individuals into 25 groups and use the 5th person in each group as a study participant.

Cluster Sampling: Researchers divide a certain population into groups, or clusters, and randomly choose several clusters in the study. For example, when examining the dining habits of residents in a certain state, you can divide these residents into clusters based on the county they live in and then use a simple random sampling method to select 8 counties for the study. Multistage sampling (also known as multistage cluster sampling) is a more complex form of cluster sampling. In multistage sampling, you draw a sample from a population using smaller and smaller groups at each stage. This method is often used to collect data from a large, geographically spread group of people in national surveys, for example.

🍁 4.53　Sources of Data

If collected by the researchers themselves and analyzed directly, the data are primary sources.

Secondary sources data are not collected by the researchers themselves.

🍁 4.54　Advantages and Limitations of Secondary Data

Although primary sources are our best option, but considering the time and cost associated with the research, we often use secondary sources.

Advantages of Secondary Data:

1) Compared to primary data, secondary data provides a time-efficient and easy-to-obtain source of information for our project by saving the time and

cost.

2) By utilizing existing databases, we may access data that would otherwise not be possible for us to collect.

3) Secondary data drawn from credible sources are sometimes more reliable than those collected by ourselves.

Limitations of Secondary Data:

1) We need more time to understand it due to the lack of familiarity with the data.

2) The data collected by others may not be ideal for solving the problems in our project.

3) The data quality of certain sources may not be guaranteed.

4) Secondary data may lack key variables.

🍁 4.55　Preparing Data

We can use different software programs to process data, such as Excel, Apache and LibreOffice.

— 第6课 —
设计问题与避免偏见

🍁 4.61 不同类型的调查

1）面对面采访

2）焦点小组

3）弹出窗口式调查

4）电话调查

5）邮寄问卷

🍁 4.62 开放式问题与封闭式问题

1）开放性问题

开放式问题是自由形式的调查问题，允许并鼓励受访者完全根据自己的知识、感受和理解进行回答。

例子：

· 跟我说说典型的一天吧。

· 告诉我您上次使用该网站的情况。

2）封闭式问题

封闭式问题将参与者限制在一组有限的可能答案中。

例子：

· 您今年多大？

· 您的职位是什么？

4.63 设计问题

我们在设计自己的问题时，需要注意下列原则：

1）保持语言简单、易读、易懂。

2）避免使用攻击性的语言或脏话。

3）不要引导受访者给出某个答案。

4）敏感性很重要：文化、性、种族等方面。

5）调查尽可能保持简短。

4.64 偏差和偏差的类型

统计偏差是指模型或统计数据不能代表总体，导致结果不准确。常见的统计偏差类型包括：

1）**抽样偏差**：由于非随机抽样而导致收集的样本有偏差。例如，你想在一所学校进行调查，而只调查了女孩。

2）**无应答偏差**：当调查参与者不愿意或无法对某个调查问题或整个调查进行回答时，就会出现无应答偏差。例如，人们挂断调查电话。

3）**应答偏差**：当调查参与者因各种各样的原因而给出错误或不精确的回答时，就会出现应答偏差。这些原因包括调查中的引导性或令人困惑的问题，例如，"您花很多时间在手机上，是吗?"

6

✦── Lesson 6 ──✦
Designing Questions and Avoiding Bias

🍁 4.61　Different Types of Surveys

1) Face-to-face interviews

2) Focus groups

3) Pop-up surveys

4) Telephone surveys

5) Mail-in questionnaires

🍁 4.62　Open vs. Closed Questions

1) Open Questions

Open questions (or open-ended questions) are free-form survey questions that allow and encourage respondents to answer in their own words completely based on their knowledge, feeling, and understanding.

Examples:

• Tell me about a typical day.

• Tell me about the last time you used the website.

2) Closed Questions

Closed questions (or closed-ended questions) restrict participants to one of a limited set of possible answers.

Examples:

• How old are you?

• What is your job title?

🍁 4.63　Designing Questions

When designing our own questions, we need to pay attention to the following principles:

1) Keep the language simple and easy to read and understand.

2) Avoid offensive or bad language.

3) Do not lead the respondents toward an answer.

4) Sensitivity is important: cultural, sexual, racial, etc.

5) Keep the survey as brief as possible.

🍁 4.64　Bias and Types of Bias

Statistical bias refers to the situation where a model or statistic is unrepresentative of the population, leading to inaccurate results. Common types of statistical bias include:

1) Sampling Bias: It refers to the collection of a biased sample caused by non-random sampling. For example, you want to conduct a survey in a school, and you only survey girls.

2) Non-response Bias: It occurs when survey participants are unwilling or unable to respond to a survey question or an entire survey. For example, people hang up on the telephone surveys.

3) Response Bias: It occurs when survey participants answer questions falsely or inaccurately for various reasons. These reasons include leading or confusing questions in the survey, for example, "You spend a lot of time on your phone, do you?"

第 5 单元

统计分析

Unit 5

Statistical Analysis

对学生的期望

　　学生应能够使用数字和图形总结来分析、解释单变量数据并得出结论。学生应该能够使用数字、图形和代数总结来分析、解释双变量数据并得出结论。学生应该理解媒体、广告业和各种职业所使用的数据管理应用软件。[1]

Expectations for Students

Students are expected to analyze, interpret, and draw conclusions from one-variable data using numerical and graphical summaries. Students should be able to analyze, interpret, and draw conclusions from two-variable data using numerical, graphical, and algebraic summaries. Students should demonstrate an understanding of the applications of data management used by the media and the advertising industry and in various occupations. [2]

---

[1][2] Ministry of Education of Ontario. *The Ontario Curriculum, Grades 11 and 12: Mathematics* [M/OL]. Toronto: Queen's Printer for Ontario, 2007: 111-122 [2024-04-29]. https://www.edu.gov.on.ca/eng/curriculum/secondary/math1112currb.pdf

— 第1课 —
直方图与数据分布

🍁 5.11 直方图

根据本课程前面的知识，我们知道直方图用于显示定量数据及其分布。有效的直方图应该具有恰当数量的矩形条，该数量取决于数据的数量。我们可以用下面的公式确定矩形条的大小：

$$矩形条大小 = \frac{数据范围}{矩形条数量}$$

🍁 5.12 数据的分布

1）对称分布

（a）单峰分布——只有一个峰值。

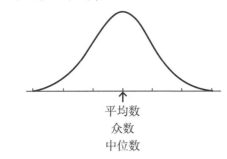

平均数
众数
中位数

（b）双峰分布——有两个峰值。

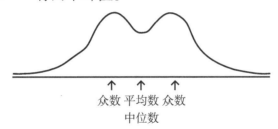

众数 平均数 众数
中位数

2）不对称分布

（a）左偏分布——最大频率在右侧。

（b）右偏分布——最大频率在左侧。

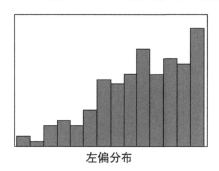
左偏分布

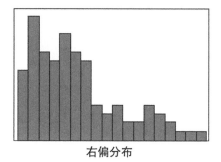
右偏分布

— Lesson 1 —
Histograms and Distribution of Data

5.11 Histograms

From previous knowledge of this course, we know that histograms are used to display quantitative data, and their distributions. An effective histogram should have the appropriate number of bins, which depends on the number of data. We can use the following formula to decide the bin size:

$$\text{bin size} = \frac{\text{range of data}}{\text{number of bins}}$$

5.12 Distribution of Data

1) Symmetrical Distribution

(a) Unimodal Distribution—There is only one peak.

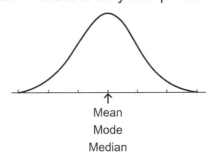

Mean
Mode
Median

(b) Bimodal Distribution—There are two peaks.

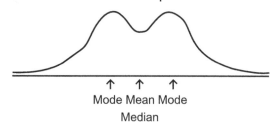

Mode Mean Mode
Median

2) Asymmetrical Distribution

(a) Left-Skewed Distribution—The greatest frequency is on the right.

(b) Right-Skewed Distribution—The greatest frequency is on the left.

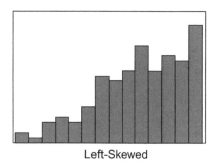

Left-Skewed

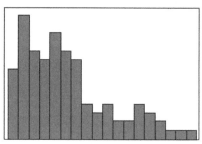

Right-Skewed

— 第 2 课 —
集中趋势的度量

🍁 5.21 什么是集中趋势的度量？

集中趋势的度量是代表一整组数据的中心点的值。集中趋势的度量主要有三种：

1）平均数——数据集里每个观测值的总和除以观测值的数量；

2）中位数——当值按升序或降序排列时，分布的中间值；

3）众数——分布中出现次数最多的值。

🍁 5.22 平均数和加权平均数

计算平均数的公式：

$$\mu = \frac{\sum_{i=1}^{n} x_i}{n}$$

μ 是平均数，n 是数字的数量。

在某些情况下，一些数字的权重比另一些的大，所以我们需要求加权平均数。加权平均数的计算公式：

$$\mu = \frac{\sum_{i=1}^{n} x_i w_i}{\sum_{i=1}^{n} w_i}$$

例子：

计算以下数据的加权平均数：

分数	96	90	95	94	88	84
权重	0.2	0.1	0.1	0.2	0.2	0.2

$$\mu = \frac{96 \times 0.2 + 90 \times 0.1 + 95 \times 0.1 + 94 \times 0.2 + 88 \times 0.2 + 84 \times 0.2}{0.2 + 0.1 + 0.1 + 0.2 + 0.2 + 0.2} = 90.9$$

如果频率表提供的是区间或范围而不是具体数字，我们应使用每个区间的中点来求平均数。

分组数据的例子：

计算以下数据的平均数：

分数	6—15	16—25	26—35	36—45	46—55	56—65
学生人数	8	12	6	14	7	3

每个区间的中点：10.5、20.5、30.5、40.5、50.5、60.5

$$\mu = \frac{10.5 \times 8 + 20.5 \times 12 + 30.5 \times 6 + 40.5 \times 14 + 50.5 \times 7 + 60.5 \times 3}{8 + 12 + 6 + 14 + 7 + 3} = 32.3$$

5.23 中位数

中位数是按顺序排列的数据集的中间值。

注意，如果数据集的值的数量是偶数，我们应求中间两个值的中点。

5.24 众数

注意，在一个数据集里，众数的个数不是固定的。因此，可以没有众数，也可以有一个众数，也可以有多个众数。

Lesson 2
Measures of Central Tendency

5.21 What Is a Measure of Central Tendency?

A measure of central tendency is a single value that represents the center point of a whole set of data. There are three main measures of central tendency:

1) Mean—the sum of the value of each observation in a data set divided by the number of observations;
2) Median—the middle value in a distribution when the values are arranged in ascending or descending order;
3) Mode—the most commonly occurring value in a distribution.

5.22 Mean and Weighted Mean

Formula to calculate the mean:

$$\mu = \frac{\sum_{i=1}^{n} x_i}{n}$$

μ is the mean, and n is the quantity of numbers.

In some cases, some numbers have more weight than others, so we want to find the weighted mean. Formula to calculate the weighted mean:

$$\mu = \frac{\sum_{i=1}^{n} x_i w_i}{\sum_{i=1}^{n} w_i}$$

Example:

Calculate the weighted mean of the following data:

Marks	96	90	95	94	88	84
Weight	0.2	0.1	0.1	0.2	0.2	0.2

$$\mu = \frac{96 \times 0.2 + 90 \times 0.1 + 95 \times 0.1 + 94 \times 0.2 + 88 \times 0.2 + 84 \times 0.2}{0.2 + 0.1 + 0.1 + 0.2 + 0.2 + 0.2} = 90.9$$

If a frequency table provides intervals or ranges rather than specific numbers, we should use the midpoint of each interval to find the mean.

Example of grouped data:

Calculate the mean of the following data:

Marks	6—15	16—25	26—35	36—45	46—55	56—65
Number of Students	8	12	6	14	7	3

Midpoint: 10.5, 20.5, 30.5, 40.5, 50.5, 60.5

$$\mu = \frac{10.5 \times 8 + 20.5 \times 12 + 30.5 \times 6 + 40.5 \times 14 + 50.5 \times 7 + 60.5 \times 3}{8 + 12 + 6 + 14 + 7 + 3} = 32.3$$

🍁 5.23 Median

The median is the middle value in a data set that has been organized sequentially.

Note that if the number of values in a data set is even, we should find the midpoint of the middle two values.

🍁 5.24 Mode

Note that in a data set, the number of modes is not set. Therefore, there can be no mode, one mode or more than one mode.

— 第 3 课 —

散布度或变异性

🍁 5.31 散布度与集中趋势

在数据管理中，散布度又称变异性，说明数据是如何分散的。在某些情况下，集中趋势不足以描述数据，我们需要其他方式来支持。

例子：

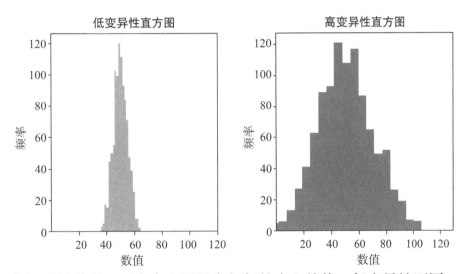

我们可以看到，两个直方图具有相似的中心趋势，但变异性不同。

学生应该理解变异性和集中趋势之间的不同。即使集中趋势相同，数据的组织方式也可能不同。

🍁 5.32 四分位距（IQR）

将数据按升序排列后，我们可以将数据分为具有相同数量的四组。将该数据集平均分为四组的数值称为四分位数。第一四分位数和第三四分位数之间的差值称为四分位距（IQR）。计算如下：

$$IQR = Q3 - Q1$$

我们还可以说四分位距是数据集的中间 50% 的范围。

注意，IQR 越大，集合中数据的散布度就越大。

箱线图是一种特殊的图表，在方格中显示四分位数，并在从方格延伸出来的两条水平线上显示最低值和最高值。

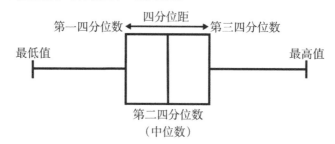

例子：

求这些分数的四分位距：1、3、3、3、4、4、4、6、6。

中位数为 4，即 Q2。

$Q1 = \dfrac{3+3}{2} = 3$ ，$Q3 = \dfrac{4+6}{2} = 5$ ，$IQR = Q3 - Q1 = 5 - 3 = 2$ ，因此四分位距为 2 分。

🍁 5.33　标准差（SD）

偏差是变量与平均数之间差异的度量。

方差是数据集合中数字之间的散布度的度量。

标准差（写为 σ）通过计算方差的平方根得出。标准差的公式为：

$$\sigma = \sqrt{\dfrac{\sum_{i=1}^{n}\left(x_i - \mu\right)^2}{N}}。$$

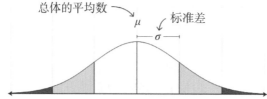

例子:

我们从花园中随机选择 5 株植物，高度分别为 38、50、46、79 和 57 厘米。计算标准差。

$$\mu = \frac{38+50+46+79+57}{5} = 54$$

$$\sigma = \sqrt{\frac{\sum_{i=1}^{n}(x_i - \mu)^2}{N}} = \sqrt{\frac{256+16+64+625+9}{5}} \approx 13.93$$

除了使用计算器解决标准差的问题外，学生还应该学习如何使用 EXCEL 或其他程序。

— Lesson 3 —
Spread or Variability

🍁 5.31 Spread vs. Central Tendency

In data management, spread, also referred to as variability, illustrates how the data are spread. In some situations, the central tendency is not enough to describe the data, and we need other ways to support.

Example:

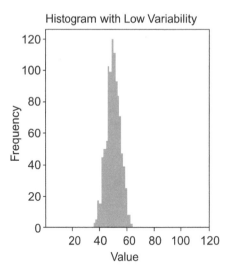

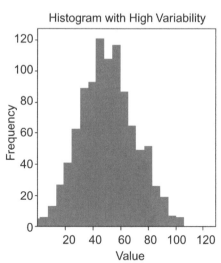

We can see that the two histograms have the similar central tendency, but the variability is different.

Students should make sense of the difference between variability and central tendency. Even if the central tendency is identical, the data may be organized differently.

🍁 5.32   Interquartile Range (IQR)

After we put the data in ascending order, we can divide the data into four groups that have the same number of variables. The values that divide the data set into four equal groups are called quartiles. The difference between the first and third quartiles is referred to as the interquartile range (IQR). The calculation is as follows:

$$IQR = Q3 - Q1$$

We can also say that the interquartile range is the range for the middle 50% of a data set.

Note that the larger the IQR is, the more spread the data is in the set.

A box plot is a special type of diagram that shows the quartiles in a box and the lowest and highest values on two horizontal lines extending from the box.

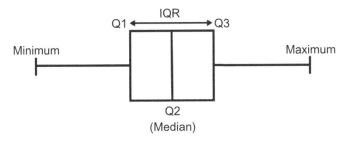

Example:

Find the IQR of these scores: 1, 3, 3, 3, 4, 4, 4, 6, 6.

The median is 4, which is Q2.

$Q1 = \dfrac{3+3}{2} = 3$, $Q3 = \dfrac{4+6}{2} = 5$, $IQR = Q3 - Q1 = 5 - 3 = 2$, so the IQR is 2 points.

🍁 5.33   Standard Deviation (SD)

Deviation is a measure of the difference between a variable and the mean.

Variance is a measure of the spread between numbers in a data set.

The standard deviation (written as σ) is calculated by taking the square root of the variance. The formula for standard deviation is:

$$\sigma = \sqrt{\frac{\sum_{i=1}^{n}\left(x_i - \mu\right)^2}{N}}.$$

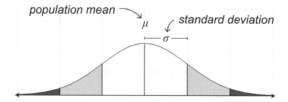

Example:

We randomly choose 5 plants from a garden, and their heights are 38, 50, 46, 79, and 57 cm. Calculate the standard deviation.

$$\mu = \frac{38 + 50 + 46 + 79 + 57}{5} = 54$$

$$\sigma = \sqrt{\frac{\sum_{i=1}^{n}\left(x_i - \mu\right)^2}{N}} = \sqrt{\frac{256 + 16 + 64 + 625 + 9}{5}} \approx 13.93$$

Apart from using the calculator to solve SD problems, students should also learn how to use EXCEL or other programs.

— 第 4 课 —
正态分布

5.41 什么是正态分布？

正态分布是一种频率分布，数据对称分布，无偏斜，并遵循钟形曲线。正态分布的一个特性是平均数、众数和中位数始终相同。

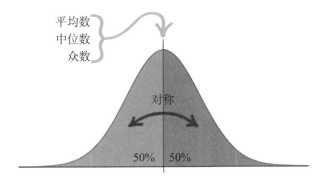

5.42 正态曲线的特征

学生记住下面的图表非常重要。

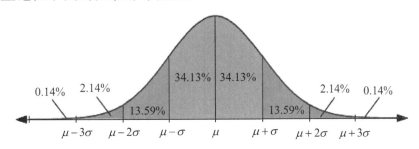

注意，68% 的数据落在 $\mu \pm \sigma$ 之间，95% 的数据落在 $\mu \pm 2\sigma$ 之间，99.7% 的数据落在 $\mu \pm 3\sigma$ 之间。

🍁 5.43 正态分布表示法

有一种描述正态分布的格式：

$$X \sim N\left(\mu, \sigma^2\right)$$

注意，σ^2 是标准差的平方。

例子：

一个城镇有 33 万成年人。他们的身高呈正态分布，平均数为 175 cm，方差为 100 cm^2。

1）用符号表示该正态分布。

$$X \sim N\left(175, 10^2\right)$$

2）什么样的身高范围有 68% 的置信度？

68% 的置信度表示身高范围是从 $\mu - \sigma$ 到 $\mu + \sigma$。因此，范围为 175-10 到 175+10 厘米，即 165 到 185 厘米。

✦ —— Lesson 4 —— ✦

Normal Distribution

🍁 5.41   What Is Normal Distribution?

Normal distribution is a frequency distribution where data is symmetrically distributed with no skewness and follows a bell curve. One particular property of normal distribution is that the mean, mode, and median are always the same.

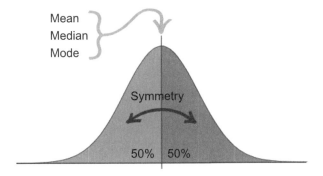

🍁 5.42   Characteristics of Normal Curve

The following graph is very important for the students to remember.

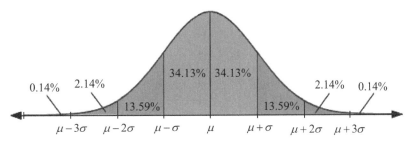

Note that 68% of the data fall between $\mu \pm \sigma$, 95% of the data fall between

$\mu \pm 2\sigma$, and 99.7% of the data fall between $\mu \pm 3\sigma$.

🍁 5.43   Normal Distribution Notation

There is a format to describe a normal distribution:

$$X \sim N\left(\mu, \sigma^2\right)$$

Note that σ^2 is the square of the standard deviation.

Example:

A town has 330,000 adults. Their heights are normally distributed with a mean of 175 cm and a variance of 100 cm^2.

a) Express the normal distribution in notation.

$$X \sim N\left(175, 10^2\right)$$

b) What range of height would have a 68% confidence?

The 68% confidence indicates that the height range is from $\mu - \sigma$ to $\mu + \sigma$. Therefore, the range would be 175−10 to 175+10 cm, which is between 165 and 185 cm.

—— 第 5 课 ——
z 分数

❦ 5.51　什么是 z 分数?

　　z 分数准确测量数据高于或低于平均数几个标准差。简单来说, z 分数让我们了解数据与平均数的距离。z 分数的另一个重要用途是它可以帮助我们比较来自不同正态分布的两个分数。

❦ 5.52　计算 z 分数

　　z 分数可以使用平均数和标准差来计算。z 分数显示给定数据距离平均数几个标准差。因此, 必须首先计算标准差, 因为 z 分数使用它来传达数据的变异性。负 z 分数值表示它位于平均数的左侧, 正 z 分数值表示它位于平均数的右侧。

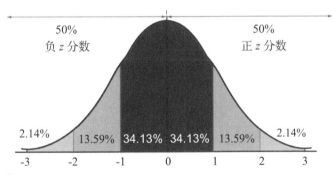

z 分数公式:

$$z = \frac{x - \mu}{\sigma}$$

例子:

假设数据集的平均数为 24, 标准差为 2, 则值 27 的 z 分数是多少?

$$z = \frac{x - \mu}{\sigma} = \frac{27 - 24}{2} = \frac{3}{2} = 1.5$$

这表明 27 比平均数高 1.5 个标准差。

我们需要的另一个重要工具是 z 表。z 表是将各种常见的 z 分数与小于或等于该 z 分数的概率关联起来的表格。计算 z 分数后，我们可以确定数据在其数据组中的百分位数。

使用 z 分数和 z 表的例子：

美国成年女子的身高呈正态分布，平均数为 63.7 英寸，标准差为 2.7 英寸。如果你随机选择一位美国成年女子，她身高超过 64 英寸的概率是多少？

$$z = \frac{x - \mu}{\sigma} = \frac{64 - 63.7}{2.7} \approx 0.11$$

参考 z 表，我们发现 $P = 0.5438$。这是分数低于或等于我们的原始分数的概率，但题目要求计算的是高于我们的原始分数的概率。因此，$1 - 0.5438 = 0.4562$。

最终答案（文字）：美国成年女子的身高超过 64 英寸的概率为 0.4562，即 45.62%。

— Lesson 5 —
Z-Scores

☘ 5.51　What Is a *Z*-Score?

A z-score measures exactly how many standard deviations above or below the mean a data point is. In simple terms, a z-score gives us an idea of how far from the mean a data point is. Another important use of a z-score is that it helps us to compare two scores from different normal distributions.

☘ 5.52　Calculating the *Z*-Score

The z-score can be calculated using the mean and standard deviation. The z-score shows the number of standard deviations a given data point lies from the mean. Therefore standard deviation must be calculated first because the z-score uses it to communicate a data point's variability. A negative z-score value means it is on the left of the mean, and a positive z-score value indicates it is on the right.

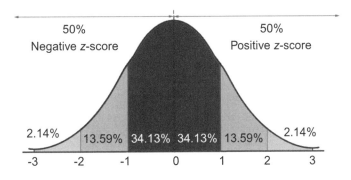

Z-score formula:

$$z = \frac{x - \mu}{\sigma}$$

Example:

What is the *z*-score of a value of 27, given a set mean of 24, and a standard deviation of 2?

$$z = \frac{x - \mu}{\sigma} = \frac{27 - 24}{2} = \frac{3}{2} = 1.5$$

This indicates that 27 is 1.5 standard deviations above the mean.

Another important tool we need is the *z*-score table. The z-score table is a table that associates the various common z-scores with the probability of being less than or equal to that z-score. After we calculate the z-score, we can determine the percentile of a data point within its data group.

Example of using the *z*-score and *z*-score table:

The heights of women in the United States are normally distributed with a mean of 63.7 inches and a standard deviation of 2.7 inches. If you randomly select a woman in the United States, what is the probability that she will be taller than 64 inches?

$$z = \frac{x - \mu}{\sigma} = \frac{64 - 63.7}{2.7} \approx 0.11$$

Referring to the *z*-score table, we find that *P* = 0.5438. This is the probability that a score will be lower than or equal to our raw score, but the question asked the proportion who would be taller. Therefore, 1 − 0.5438 = 0.4562.

Final Answer (in words): The probability that a woman in the U.S. would be taller than 64 inches is 0.4562, or 45.62%.

━━ 第6课 ━━

数学指数

🍁 5.61 什么是指数？

指数是用于比较不同情况下测量的具有相同特征的两个量的数字。

🍁 5.62 指数示例

体重指数（BMI）是用来衡量人体胖瘦程度的一个指数。

$$BMI = \frac{m}{h^2}（m指质量，以千克为单位；h指身高，以米为单位）$$

例子：

某女性的身高是 1.6 m，体重是 80 kg，计算 BMI。

$$BMI = \frac{m}{h^2} = \frac{80}{1.6^2} = 31.25$$

长打率（SLG）用于衡量棒球运动员的表现。

$$SLG = \frac{垒打数}{打数}$$

例子：

一名球员击球 613 次，取得 60 个一垒打、34 个二垒打、4 个三垒打和 58 个本垒打，求 SLG。

$$SLG = \frac{垒打数}{打数}$$

$$= \frac{60 + 34 \times 2 + 4 \times 3 + 58 \times 4}{613} = \frac{372}{613} \approx 0.607$$

　　可以为任何关于两个数量的比较创建指数。加拿大商业和金融部门广泛使用两种专用指数：消费价格指数和标准普尔 / 多伦多证券交易所综合指数。

— Lesson 6 —
Mathematical Indices

5.61 What Is an Index?

An index is a number used to compare two quantities sharing the same characteristic as measured under different circumstances.

5.62 Index Examples

Body Mass Index (BMI) is an index that is used to measure a person's leanness or corpulence.

$$\text{BMI} = \frac{m}{h^2} \left(m \text{ is mass in } kg, h \text{ is height in } m \right)$$

Example:

A woman is 1.6 m tall and weighs 80 kg. Calculate the BMI.

$$\text{BMI} = \frac{m}{h^2} = \frac{80}{1.6^2} = 31.25$$

Slugging Percentage (SLG) is used to measure a baseball player's performances.

$$\text{SLG} = \frac{\text{total bases}}{\text{at-bats}}$$

Example:

A player goes to bat 613 times and results in 60 singles, 34 doubles, 4 triples and 58 home runs. Determine the SLG.

$$\text{SLG} = \frac{\text{total bases}}{\text{at-bats}}$$

$$= \frac{60 + 34 \times 2 + 4 \times 3 + 58 \times 4}{613} = \frac{372}{613} \approx 0.607$$

Indices can be created for any comparison of two quantities. Two specialized indices are widely used across the business and financial sectors of Canada: the Consumer Price Index and the S&P/TSX Composite Index.

练习题与参考答案

Exercises and
Suggested Answers

Organization of Data

Multiple Choice Questions: *Circle the choice that best completes the statement or answers the question.*

1. Which of the following statements is true about the collection of data?

    A. The usage of information helps to save both time and money.

    B. The usage of primary data helps to save both time and money.

    C. The usage of secondary data helps to save both time and money.

    D. The usage of data helps to save both time and money.

2. Which of the following methods is most effective in minimizing misrepresentation and misunderstanding?

    A. Using questionnaires

    B. Holding personal interactions

    C. Writing e-mails

    D. Using telephones

3. Which of the following statements is correct?

    A. Once the questions are ready, it is advisable that a pilot survey of the questionnaire is conducted with a small group.

    B. Once the questions are ready, it is advisable that a survey of the questionnaire is conducted with a small group.

    C. Once the questions are ready, it is advisable that an observation of the questionnaire is conducted with a small group.

    D. None of the above

4. Which of the following statements is true about the lottery method?

    A. The lottery method is also known as random sampling.

    B. The lottery method is also known as population sampling.

    C. The lottery method is also known as non-random sampling.

D. The lottery method is also known as sampling.

5. Which of the following statements about sampling errors is accurate?

A. The difference between the sampling estimate and the corresponding parameter is not a type of sampling error.

B. Sampling bias is not a type of sampling error.

C. Data entry errors are not a type of sampling error.

D. Non-response errors are not a type of sampling error.

6. Which of the following statements about the spatial classification of data is true?

A. In terms of spatial classification, data is classified on the basis of geographical location.

B. In terms of spatial classification, data is classified on the basis of time series.

C. In terms of spatial classification, data is classified on the basis of quantitative classification.

D. In terms of spatial classification, data is classified on the basis of chronological classification.

7. Which of the following statements correctly describes the process of classifying raw data?

A. Analysis is a comprehensive method that helps in the classification of raw data.

B. Frequency distribution is a comprehensive method that helps in the classification of raw data.

C. Distribution is a comprehensive method that helps in the classification of raw data.

D. Information is a comprehensive method that helps in the classification of raw data.

8. Which of the following statements is true about class intervals?

A. The exclusive class intervals are used on a frequent basis in the case of continuous variables.

    B. The inclusive class intervals are used on a frequent basis in the case of continuous variables.

    C. The offline class intervals are used on a frequent basis in the case of continuous variables.

    D. The online class intervals are used on a frequent basis in the case of continuous variables.

9. Which of the following statements about continuous variables is accurate?

    A. The pie charts are drawn only for continuous variables.

    B. The bar diagrams are drawn only for continuous variables.

    C. The histograms are drawn only for continuous variables.

    D. The frequency curves are drawn only for continuous variables.

10. Which of the following statements about the collection of data is true?

    A. The main purpose behind the collection of data is to show the evidence required to reach a clear solution for the problem.

    B. The main purpose behind the collection of data is to show the movement required to reach a clear solution for the problem.

    C. The main purpose behind the collection of data is to show the design required to reach a clear solution for the problem.

    D. The main purpose behind the collection of data is to show the figures required to reach a clear solution for the problem.

11. Which of the following is a database of first-hand information?

    A. Primary data

    B. Secondary data

    C. Both A and B are correct.

    D. Both A and B are incorrect.

12. Which of the following statements is correct?

    A. A pilot survey is extremely useful in providing preliminary data about the survey.

B. An airline survey is extremely useful in providing preliminary data about the survey.

C. A mailing survey is extremely useful in providing preliminary data about the survey.

D. A shipping survey is extremely useful in providing preliminary data about the survey.

13. How often is the census carried out in Canada?

A. Once every ten years

B. Once every twenty years

C. Once every seven years

D. Once every five years

14. Which of the following statements about sampling is correct?

A. A good sample helps to provide reasonably accurate information about the population.

B. A good sample helps to provide totally accurate information about the population.

C. A good sample does not provide reasonably accurate information about the population.

D. None of the above

15. It is possible to _____ the magnitude of sampling error if we take a _____ sample.

A. increase, larger

B. decrease, larger

C. decrease, smaller

D. None of the above

Suggested Answers

1–5 C B A A A   6–10 A B A D A   11–15 A A D A B

Statistical Analysis

Section 1 Multiple Choice Questions: *Circle the choice that best completes the statement or answers the question.*

1. For the following density curve, what percent of the observations lie between 0.2 and 3.8?
   A. 10%
   B. 20%
   C. 28%
   D. 68%
   E. 72%

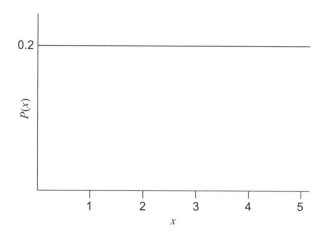

2. The 35th percentile of a population is the number x so
   A. 35% of the population scores are above x.
   B. 65% of the population scores are above x.
   C. 35% of the population scores equal x.
   D. x is 35% of the population median.
   E. x is 35% of the population mean.

3. Consider the following cumulative relative frequency graph of the scores of students in an introductory statistics course:

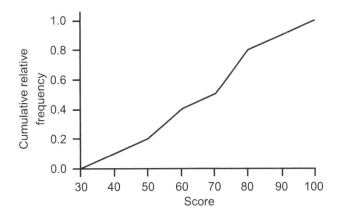

A grade of C or C+ is assigned to a student who scores between 55 and 70. The percentage of students who obtained a grade of C or C+ is

A. 15%.

B. 20%.

C. 25%.

D. 30%.

E. 50%.

4. The distribution of household incomes in a small town is strongly skewed to the right. The mean income is \$42,000 and the standard deviation is \$24,000. The Ames family's household income is \$60,000. The z-score for the Ames family's income is

A. −0.75.

B. 0.3.

C. 0.75.

D. 0.86.

E. none of these, because z-score cannot be used unless the distribution is normal.

5. A sample was taken of the salaries of 20 employees of a large company. The following are the salaries (in thousands of dollars) for this year. For convenience, the data are ordered.

28	31	34	35	37	41	42	42	42	47
49	51	52	52	60	61	67	72	75	77

Suppose each employee in the company receives a $3,000 raise for next year (each employee's salary is increased by $3,000). The mean salary for the employees will

A. be unchanged.

B. increase by $3,000.

C. be multiplied by $3,000.

D. decrease by $3,000.

E. increase by $150.

6. The birth weights at a local hospital have a normal distribution with a mean of 110 oz and a standard deviation of 15 oz. The proportion of infants with birth weights under 95 oz is about

A. 15.9%.

B. 2.5%.

C. 34.1%.

D. 50%.

E. 84.1%.

7. Using the standard normal table, we can find that the area under the standard normal curve corresponding to $z > -1.22$ is

A. 0.1112.

B. 0.1151.

C. 0.4129.

D. 0.8849.

E. 0.8888.

8. The scores on a university examination are normally distributed with a mean of 62 and a standard deviation of 11. If the bottom 5% of students will fail the course, what is the lowest mark that a student can have and still be awarded a passing grade?

A. 40

B. 43

C. 44

D. 57

E. 62

9. The time to complete a standardized exam is approximately normal with a mean of 70 minutes and a standard deviation of 10 minutes. How much time should be given to complete the exam so that 80% of the students will complete the exam in the time given?

A. 61.6 minutes

B. 78.4 minutes

C. 79.8 minutes

D. 84 minutes

E. 92.8 minutes

10. When a basketball player makes a pass to a teammate who then scores, he earns an "assist." Below is a normal probability plot for the number of assists earned by all players in the National Basketball Association during the 2023 regular season.

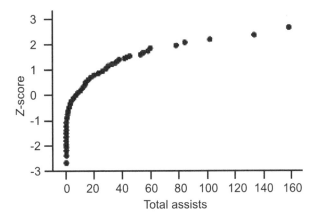

Which of the following statements about the shape of this distribution is true?

A. The distribution is normal.

B. The distribution is approximately normal.

C. The distribution is roughly symmetric.

D. The distribution has no potential outliers.

E. The distribution is skewed.

Section 2 Short Answer Questions

1. A real estate company compiled data on the prices at which 35 homes sold during one month in a county in New Jersey. A histogram and some summary statistics from Minitab for the home prices are given below. (Note that home prices are in thousands of dollars.)

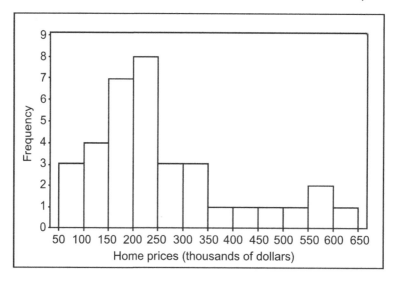

Descriptive Statistics: Home Prices

Variable	N	Mean	SE Mean	StDev	Minimum	Q1	Median	Q3	Maximum
Home Prices	35	260.8	24.6	145.6	80.0	165.0	220.0	307.0	626.0

What was the "typical" price for a home in this county during the month in which these data were collected? Justify your answer.

2. 98 women and 225 men participated in a five kilometer road race. Below are the summary statistics from Minitab on their times in the race.

Descriptive Statistics: Women and Men

Variable	N	Mean	StDev	Minimum	Q1	Median	Q3	Maximum
Women	98	28.891	6.481	17.717	24.229	26.917	32.525	48.800
Men	225	24.758	5.026	15.050	21.117	24.050	27.608	48.417

Santiago finished in 51st place among the men, with a time of 20.9 minutes. Keisha finished 33rd among women, with a time of 25.2 minutes. Use percentiles and z-scores to compare Santiago's and Keisha's relative standing among men and women, respectively.

3. Find the proportion of observations from a standard normal distribution that satisfies $0.51 < z < 2.84$. Sketch the normal curve and shade the area under the curve that is the answer to the question.

Suggested Answers

Section 1

1–5 E B B C B   6–10 A E C B E

Section 2

1. $220,000—the median is the best measure of the center of a skewed distribution.

2. Santiago's percentile is (50/225) × 100 ≈ 22 and his z-score is (20.9 – 24.758)/5.026 ≈ –0.77.

   Keisha's percentile is (32/98) × 100 ≈ 33 and her z-score is (25.2 – 28.891)/6.481 ≈ –0.57.

   Since lower finish times are better, Santiago had a better relative standing among men than Keisha had among women.

3. Proportion = 0.3027.

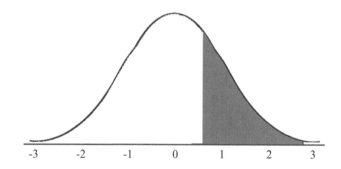

词汇表

Glossary

- Asymmetrical Distribution   不对称分布
- Bar Graph   柱状图
- Binomial Distribution   二项式分布
- Binomial Experiment   二项式实验
- Binomial Probability   二项式概率
- Binomial Theorem   二项式定理
- Body Mass Index   体重指数
- Box Plot   箱线图
- Circle Graph   圆形图
- Closed Question   封闭式问题
- Cluster Sampling   整群抽样
- Combination   组合
- Complement   补集
- Conditional Probability   条件概率
- Continuous Data   连续数据
- Dependent Variable   因变量
- Deviation   偏差
- Discrete Data   离散数据
- Expected Value   期望值
- Experimental Probability   实验概率
- Exponent Law   指数运算法则
- Factorial   阶乘
- Frequency Table   频率表
- Histogram   直方图
- Independent Event   独立事件
- Independent Variable   自变量

- Interquartile Range   四分位距
- Intersection   交集
- Left-Skewed   左偏分布
- Line of Best Fit   最佳拟合线
- Linear Correlation   线性相关
- Mathematical Index   数学指数
- Mean   平均数
- Measure of Central Tendency   集中趋势的度量
- Median   中位数
- Mode   众数
- Multiplicative Principle   乘法原理
- Multistage Sampling   多阶段抽样
- Mutually Exclusive Events   互斥事件
- Non-probability Sampling   非概率抽样
- Non-response Bias   无应答偏差
- Normal Approximation   正态近似
- Normal Distribution   正态分布
- Open Question   开放式问题
- Order of Operations   运算顺序
- Outcome Table   结果表
- Pascal's Triangle   杨辉三角形
- Permutation   排列
- Pictograph   象形图画
- Pie Chart   饼状图
- Probability   概率
- Probability Distribution   概率分布

- Probability Notation   概率表示法
- Probability Sampling   概率抽样
- Qualitative Data   定性数据
- Quantitative Data   定量数据
- Random Sampling   随机抽样
- Response Bias   应答偏差
- Right-Skewed   右偏分布
- Sampling Bias   抽样偏差
- Scatter Plot   散点图
- Simple Random Sampling   简单随机抽样
- Simulation   模拟
- Slugging Percentage   长打率
- Standard Deviation   标准差
- Stem-and-Leaf Plot   茎叶图
- Stratified Sampling   分层抽样
- Symmetrical Distribution   对称分布
- Systematic Sampling   系统抽样
- Theoretical Probability   理论概率
- Thesis   研究问题
- Tree Diagram   树形图
- Union   并集
- Variability   变异性
- Variable   变量
- Variance   方差
- Venn Diagram   维恩图
- Z-Score z 分数

鸣谢山东东营胜利新西兰学校